MINDBLOWING

J. P. CODNIA

WestBow Press books may be ordered through booksellers or by contacting:

WestBow Press
A Division of Thomas Nelson & Zondervan
1663 Liberty Drive
Bloomington, IN 47403
www.westbowpress.com
1 (866) 928-1240

ISBN: 978-1-4908-9785-1 (sc)
ISBN: 978-1-4908-9786-8 (e)

Print information available on the last page.

WestBow Press rev. date: 03/22/2016

To my dear daughter Michelle

SOAKING UP MOSCOW

For most people, a late January morning may not seem appealing enough to travel to Moscow facing – among other things – the incredible winter chill. But this is precisely what sets Liz McGillan and Wanda Newtowne apart from many people. They are determined to sacrifice their comfort zone, accepting to postpone time and again their right to enjoy life like ordinary girls in consideration of other things. Gifted with inquisitive minds, Liz and Wanda are led to search through intricate issues of life, discovering and discerning, separating truth from myth, much like in a competition where pretenders are separated from contenders to find a winner. In this sense, the girls have a job like no other, one that demands hard work but allows them to meet amazing people who offer them support, resources, and contacts necessary to make it in the world.

For months, Liz and Wanda exchanged all sorts of likes/dislikes online with Irina Baranchuk, a Moscow resident the girls considered as close as a next-door neighbour. And they were thrilled to receive Irina's invitation to her wedding. The pair had a special interest in visiting Russia, a nation rich in history and culture, and a mix of heroes and villains. Liz and Wanda longed to see it all first hand.

Irina's flat was big enough to accommodate her two guests, and as customary in that part of the world, she arranged for them to feel really comfortable with the help of things like a pair of mobile phones and a list of all essential numbers/addresses. There was also a basic course in Russian that would let the visitors be understood when interacting with non-English-speaking Russians.

On the day of the girls' arrival, Irina had a long schedule: a couple of tests at the university –definitely important being only three months from graduation – and then a meeting with her marriage counselor, who was helping with the couple's preparations. Irina Baranchuk is the kind of girl who knows the value of always doing the best; whatever the situation or endeavour, she gave her best. At twenty-three, Irina shows qualities that make her the right candidate for a

Russian network specialising in international affairs, and her certification would make it official. This somehow would tie in perfectly with having her best friends from cyberworld there.

Just outside Moscow's international airport, a group of college students gathered to express their satisfaction for a decision made by the European Union to ban the theory of creationism from schools. These students were a mob of loud individuals and held posters with the likes of Lenin, Stalin, Hitler, and Darwin, referring to them as if they all belonged to a team seeking the betterment of humankind by selecting certain persons to represent those "more fit" to survive. Liz and Wanda were shocked and confused when they saw the crowd. But then it dawned on them that history tends to repeat itself due to a lack of knowledge.

Basically, hunger for power and domination of others, as well as a desire for unlimited wealth, has always played a part in the destruction that affected even the most prosperous nations. It can be reduced to a very short sentence: power corrupts. People need leaders, but corruption has a way of getting in there. Sometimes something relatively small starts a painful chapter in history, like a forbidden passion or the curiosity to find out what will happen.

Liz and Wanda studied history and knew how the Russian revolution of 1917 took place. They knew about the horrors that followed, even decades after the change in government from a royal family to a dictatorship. The new government was responsible for the massive extermination of Russians declared guilty of crimes against the state. Such crimes included being non-supporters of the communist government, or acknowledging their faith in the God of the Bible, a major offence. The government had the power to treat the people of the USSR however it wanted, because there were no rights or freedoms. There was no protection from the state, not even inside people's dwellings. The state could order someone's home to be raided at any time of the day or night under suspicion of violating the obligated allegiance to the communist regime. Fear began to take over. Families were ripped apart as officials arrested increasing numbers of men, who were relocated to concentration camps in Siberia or executed.

The feeling of uncertainty was not all that affected the majority of Russians. There was an actual level of inhumanity against them. Lenin used the famine of 1921–22 as a tool to send a strong message to the people. Many families were forced to go without food. Months passed, with bodies piling up. The communist government blocked relief efforts organised by an American commission simply because it was an American effort.

The new communist government quickly gained control of what its subjects did and believed. The political situation in the USSR resembled that of the Germans at the time. Officials in both countries believed they had the right to use persons for experiments to help the country. So a philosophical movement originating with Nietzsche, Freud, and others contributed to a new plan to look for ways to achieve a better human being and a better race. Many experiments took place, including ones using drugs and methods of mind invasion. The dreadful results were seen as a small price to pay for the sake of the cause. Though somehow related to Darwin's quest for answers, unlike Darwin, they had a political agenda. For Germany and the USSR, the goal was to be feared as the most powerful country in the world.

Charles Darwin was a scientist dedicated to studying plants and lower animals. Liz and Wanda, being familiar with Darwin, realised he did not belong in the same group as the early-twentieth-century dictators, because Darwin, as a naturalist, spent his life studying and classifying countless species of the vegetable and animal kingdoms instead of killing people and ruining lives. So it seemed as though this was a case of mistaken identity, or twisted identity, which was often conveniently used by some to push their rather unorthodox agendas. This called to mind two tragic incidents in America – one in Colorado and the other in Virginia – where the perpetrators openly shared their strong views about the right of some to live and the duty for others to be killed. Liz and Wanda felt disturbed.

As they approached their destination, a passer-by handed the girls a flyer. It read,

Evolution by Purpose: A lecture by Jacob Kodnia

The lecture would be given in Russian and English. The event was scheduled for later that day and not far from Irina's apartment. Considering the bad taste of Darwin's theory in the girls' mouths – or the way many people took to it – Liz and Wanda decided the lecture was a must-see.

THE LECTURE

A WARM SHOWER AND A CHANGE of clothes were just what the two travellers needed to feel ready for an interesting evening in Moscow. The lecture by a Jacob Kodnia was more than a cultural event to entertain visitors; it would afford audiences an opportunity to explore the platform upon which a settlement could be built based on a controversial, self-explosive topic. As for Liz and Wanda, they perceived it as an effort to restore something damaged, perhaps through some missing link that would enable the human mind, with its intellect, to decipher or interpret an enigmatic subject.

The auditorium was crowded when the pair arrived just before 3.00. The lecture would stop for a fifteen-minute break at 4.30 and, after that, the conclusion. Liz and Wanda found two seats close to the left side of the stage. Jacob came out and introduced himself. He had a device that provided visual information in slides, along with a sophisticated electronic recorded system which read bits of information in Russian and English. The audio was programmed with enough time for listeners to follow in one language or the other. He had obviously spent a great deal of time preparing the material needed for the lecture.

Jacob was in his seventies. As a boy, he had a difficult life coping with the sheer fear of Stalin's troops and wondering where he would settle. Jacob remembered his uncle and aunt, who was with child, escaping the USSR dressed to look like an old couple. They went to Poland and then to Great Britain by boat. They could not stay there once reports warned them the Soviets had sent spies to England to track and eliminate dissidents. Jacob spent time in the United Kingdom before moving to Poland with cousins. After a long time, he returned to his native Ukraine.

On this evening in Moscow, however, Jacob was only to talk about evolution, to which he added the distinctive remark "by purpose." This meant the evolution process did not occur the way it was usually taught, by using a tree to show all life forms evolved from a single cell, and somehow, countless groups of plants and animals appeared. Jacob gave credit to some scientists whose contributions in the field of microbiology proved quite valuable. Thanks to them we know the principle of irreducible complexity is real; the structures that make up the cells in our bodies verify that certain components in the body are of no use at all unless combined with others. Being a remarkably honest man, Darwin anticipated this issue of multicomplex structures when he studied the eye, so he acknowledged certain things were not in line with the natural selection process as he introduced it to the world in 1859. Another problem with the theory of evolution –also recognised by Darwin – is the fossil record. If the tree of evolution was accurate, there should be transitional bones, verifying that and many are needed. Darwin believed that at some point in the future, such transitional bones would be found. So far, however, they have not. This is odd, for there are thousands of bones recovered that correspond to a huge variety of dinosaurs from around the world. Whether it be skeletons or fossilised rocks, it is true the creatures existed, though there are no skeletons actually linking apes to humankind, only some limited similarities.

Jacob stated the problem in accepting Darwin's natural selection, or its affiliate sexual selection, is not whether that agency exists – because it does – but how it works and how far it goes. He cited Darwin's 1871 book, *The Descent of Man*. It was in it that Darwin introduced a substantial amount of material based on contemplative speculation. Jacob explained a possible cause. Unlike Darwin's first book, *The Origin of Species, The Descent of Man* contains numerous ideas and collaborations from people who corresponded with Charles Darwin. They sent him articles, and he cites them one by one. Hence readers become recipients of certain bits of information that did not originate with the author. This leaves room for inferences as they are acknowledged in the book. Jacob specifically cited the part of the book in which Darwin wrote the reason humans have nipples is that at some time in the past, some apelike ancestors – females and males – had the capacity to nurse their offspring. In *The Origin of Species,* Darwin defined the agent he called 'sexual selection', indicating certain features or structures are only for ornamental purposes. Who is to say that a man's nipples are not on his chest just for looks then? "Is it really easier to think that two million years ago a male ancestor produced milk and just gave it to his babies? This is 100 percent speculation."

Jacob cited another example, using the human ear. As he had with males' nipples, he said ears were mainly for improving one's appearance. Then he brought up another feature, the eyebrows, telling his audience something not contemplated in *The Descent of Man.* According to Jacob, eyebrows are not simply for ornamental purposes but are a communication tool as well. Jokingly he added, "If you don't believe me, ask Selena Gomez." Some who heard that laughed in agreement.

SCIENCE OR MYTHOLOGY

With only a few minutes before taking a break, Jacob offered two distinct patterns that can be observed in Darwin's writings. One was characterised by extensive research on plants, insects, birds, and sea life; discovering and sharing amazing things with the world, For example, he shared the hydra, an animal that may be turned inside out. The exterior surface would then digest, and the stomach respire. Darwin noticed that one organ may be capable of performing two functions or two different organs made to perform the same function, as in the case with certain fish. Darwin clearly wanted answers for himself as well as for others, so he invested many years investigating and studying plants and animals from such remote places as the Galapagos Islands, and Ushuaia, and comparing them with species found in Europe, America, Africa, Asia, and Australia.

The other side has more to do with his reliance on outsiders, that is, individuals who simply corresponded with Darwin from other cities. It makes research more complicated when a number of people casually exchange views. This seems to be the scenario in Darwin's life, when he was led to "infer that earlier forefathers of man were probably furnished great canine teeth," and that "progenitors of man changed from quadrupeds into bipeds." In his latter years, Darwin became more influenced by the opinions of others, which in turn proved more acceptable in his view of how life forms evolved, particularly how human life originated. Instead of going to places to see for himself every possible clue in case a match or evidence were found, Darwin decided to infer, adding to his thoughts the word "probably." Jacob's description of Darwin's life circumstances also impressed the audience, and even those who understood the division between creationism and evolution appeared to be ignorant of important factors concerning the works of Charles Darwin.

Jacob spoke with clarity against the theory students are obligated to accept as if it were fact, especially that some two million years ago a type of ape began to separate itself from its ancestors by losing the tail, walking on twos, and becoming divested of hair. Jacob also spoke against the idea of Darwin being called an evil or blasphemous man. He urged his audience to read the author's books and learn about his life for better understanding. Darwin was neither perfect nor a demon, but a man who left a legacy which includes – in his own words – the task given to future generations to discern the things he conceived and the views that were to be proven erroneous.

MEETING JACOB KODNIA

T HE RECESS AT 4.30 PROMPTED Liz and Wanda to meet the host. Jacob had already begun to walk down the hallway behind the curtain when he heard the girls calling out to him. "Mr. Kodnia … Mr. Kodnia … could we have a word with you, please?"

Jacob turned around, nodded, and walked back towards the callers. Liz spoke first. "Your lecture is really impressive, sir. We wanted to let you know we have been talking about things like evolution for years. And now, for first time, we get to see that there are so many elements … enough evidence to do away with certain myths."

Jacob answered, "Thank you, Miss. I am glad to know that not everyone is buying into all the stories they hear in science class."

At that, Wanda said, "Oh, we know what you mean, sir – the big-bang, the breakup of Pangaea, the extinction of dinosaurs, among other hot-button topics that are often explained with a large dose of science fiction."

Jacob grinned. "You two are certainly wise beyond your years, friends, but be careful not to act carelessly, being too outspoken. Pray for being at the right place at the right time, because timing usually defines the level of success on a mission."

"Thank you, Mr. Kodnia", both girls replied. "We will keep that in mind. So nice to meet you."

"Pleased to have met you both." With a handshake, Liz and Wanda went outside the auditorium.

ESCORTED OUT

WHILE JACOB WAS DRINKING TEA in the break room, a man approached him and identified himself as Inspector Igor Trotsky, from the special squad of the Moscow police. He had just received the order to take Jacob away under suspicion of disturbing the peace by inciting the public to disorderly conduct. Inspector Trotsky handed the summons for Jacob to read, and deciding not to handcuff the elderly man, he led Jacob outside the building to a waiting patrol car. Jacob quietly got in the car, and they drove off.

Liz and Wanda were out viewing the city from the sidewalk when they caught sight of the incident. Liz began to scream, but it was no use. After a moment of shock, Wanda told her, "Don't panic, Liz, I think I've got an idea. I don't believe Jacob will be detained for long. Listen." Liz nodded, and the pair began to try to work out why Jacob would be taken away.

They quickly decided to send an SOS to Irina, who immediately realised the man needed legal help. Irina told them she would contact an attorney in anticipation of the arraignment Jacob would face by the next day. She understood the situation, and though the case looked rather weak, she knew it would be best to have someone there to clear the charges. Irina explained, "Sometimes a case in itself lacks weight but then prosecutors throw in technicalities to add weight and make it look ugly in court."

Liz and Wanda were nervous. They related to Irina their experience that morning at the airport, and Jacob's arrest didn't exactly help them stay calm.

After hearing about what went on at Moscow's international airport, Irina sensed her friends could use some support. "I'm at the university pub with my fiancé, Sergei, but I will be back home in less than an hour, and we will talk … the four of us. Don't worry."

LIZ AND WANDA SEEK HELP

THE PHONE CONVERSATION WITH IRINA was comforting. The girls felt more confident that a solution would come. And though it was strange, they felt the incident was expected, much like noise or fireworks can be expected on New Year's Eve.

Irina and Sergei met their guests, and talked for hours, with a bit of vodka first followed by plenty of mocha. The group started jotting down ideas for a course of action. Someone mentioned the imminent big event – the Winter Olympics – in Sochi, a city by the Black Sea. A quick search online revealed some of the athletes were in Moscow, preparing and training. Wanda proposed a plan based on that. "If we could talk to some of those athletes, I know it would create some leverage, and given the fact that it is happening at the time of a huge international event, officials here would have to be cautious not to get involved in a mess with global repercussions."

Liz agreed. "Jacob was only inviting people to see for themselves, to examine both the creation and evolution theories, because neither are completely black or white ... and ..." Liz went blank and was unable to speak.

Irina and Sergei asked if she was all right. "Must have been the vodka", the couple commented.

But Wanda said, "I know that face. Liz was shocked by something she must have thought of just now. Let's give her a moment, and she will tell us." The three of them smiled as Liz grasped something extremely important. The solution to the old problem between evolution and creation was not to insist on their discrepancies but to examine what they had in common. All in favour, the plan was ready.

The next morning, Wanda sat down to get information about the athletes who were to be in the Olympics at Sochi – names, nationalities, sports and contact agent if available. The list was long at first, but as Wanda went through it all, she narrowed it down to just a handful. The good news was the small group could be available for a chat with her. Wanda gave Liz the information about a girl from Ukraine, who happened to be in Moscow to practice figure skating. And while Liz went to meet the athlete at the rink, Wanda had five others to see, three of whom seemed likely to be of help. Meanwhile, Irina and Sergei headed to magistrate court to find out the status of Jacob's case and talk to the counsel there.

Wanda Newtowne introduced herself to a couple of girls who were anxious to start a race. The three met at the track, and though less than enthusiastic, the two athletes shook hands with the visitor. "Hey, I'm Victoria, representing South Africa. This is Abalyah, from the Middle East. We compete, but we're also friends. Are you a reporter, Wanda?"

With a brief hesitation, Wanda answered, "No, I am not. But I'm working on something important, and I came here hoping to have a few minutes with you two to talk. By the way, I am a social worker." The athletes nodded, and Wanda told them about what she had witnessed the day before.

Victoria asked, "Is it really bad? Scandals are not rare in cosmopolitan places, you know?"

The situation seemed difficult to explain, but Wanda tried. "True, but I'm afraid this is one of those showdowns with a political agenda, because it's intended to force people to accept the theory of evolution at face value, without even a chance to see if certain ideas proposed are correct or not. That is an issue Darwin did not want."

Abalyah remained silent, listening. Victoria, however, engaged in the conversation. "I never read what Darwin wrote, so I don't really know what is in his books that caused so much trouble. I do remember in my childhood people had arguments associated with apartheid folks, who teased coloured people with stupid comments, like, 'Dark-skinned persons are behind in the evolutionary scale.' Never did appreciate that sort of thing, really, because the person's character counts a great deal."

"That's right," Wanda agreed. "And in the end, reality shows there is no such thing as supremacy based on skin tone alone … but the efforts made to become a better person, with better standards and values to help themselves and others."

"Like Nelson Mandela, Martin Luther King, Robert Kennedy", Victoria added.

"Spot on", Wanda concurred.

Victoria continued, trying to establish what to do. "Did you find anyone else willing to help yet?"

"Yes, actually. The college girl who invited us here is helping with the legal aspects right now. And …" Wanda felt some kind of inspiration. "You know, Victoria, you are giving me an idea that I think will be very cool. I just need to check on something with my best friend. What I would truly appreciate from you would be to let me call you and Abalyah and maybe some other athletes for a photo shoot if you happen to be in Moscow for a few more days." Wanda was very excited by then, but she couldn't quite share with Victoria all that popped up in her head, because she had something to verify first.

"That shouldn't be a problem. We have to stay for at least a whole week. Call me to let me know about that photograph, all right? Here's my number."

Victoria's kindness made the day for Wanda, who promised to call her the next day. She anticipated the photo shoot she was thinking of would be at Irina's college.

The rink was almost empty when Liz arrived. She stood at the entrance for a moment, and as she caught sight of Tatiana, she marvelled at the work that goes into the Olympics. Liz saw a small group watching the girl's routine from the opposite end of the rink and discerned they were from the Ukranian team. Tatiana's good looks combined well with her skills as she glided gracefully on the ice. After about ten minutes, Tatiana beckoned Liz. "Hi, you must be Liz. My coach, Olga, told me you were coming to talk about a friend of yours, who spoke the truth and got the axe."

Liz couldn't have put it better. "That's right, Tatiana. It's nice to meet you. I've been watching for a while, enjoying the practice."

"Great! At least somebody is", Tatiana scoffed. "From where I'm standing, it can be a pain. But that's a story for another day. What can I do for you … I mean for Jacob?"

Just as Tatiana said those words, Liz felt her phone vibrate. It was Wanda, asking her to get the skater to join the other athletes for the photo shoot at Irina's university Liz sighed and said, "Perfect timing." By then, Olga had joined the conversation, and it shifted to politics, Darwin, and the Sochi 2014 Olympics. Liz arranged with Olga and Tatiana to meet in one week. Swaying to the sound of music, the girl resumed her practice.

Liz McGillan called Wanda, confirming some good news. "The girl and her coach said yes, Wanda, so we'll meet again at Irina's college. By the way, could you be more specific? When you called me, you said you'd explain later. So what's the plan?"

"Sorry, Liz. Right now I'm in the middle of a fast search. Just like you had an inspired moment yesterday, something occurred to me while I was talking to the girls at the track. It could really work, and I mean as evidence to use in court. But give me a couple of hours to make sure it is good. All right, I'm on my way to meet another candidate to join our crusade. Her name is Xuang Chang, and she is a gymnast. I am hoping she will be flexible in other areas." Liz laughed.

Xuang Chang had been busy practicing risky flips and landings. Her trainer answered the door when Wanda knocked and led her through the gym to see Xuang. A man with an outgoing personality chatted with Wanda until the young Chinese competitor completed practice. This was the first Olympics for Xuang. After a winning streak at events across China, she became the logical choice for Sochi 2014. Despite her age, she knew a great deal about sacrifices, hard work, and not being able to make her own decisions. Xuang and her trainer agreed to stop at Irina's college for the photograph after Wanda assured them it would not be used to promote one country as better than the others. This would be strictly about science, not politics, so it was easy for to comply with the trainer's condition.

Irina and Sergei were in court, getting information on the case. The counsel had met with Jacob and the judge. The important news was that charges would not be dropped, so a hearing must take place for an opportunity to clear Jacob Kodnia. On the bright side, Jacob was on house arrest instead of rotting in a cell. The hearing, set for the third of March, should give the coalition group enough time to prepare. Irina and Sergei's wedding, only a few days before the trial, would require a minor adjustment. When they later spoke with Liz and Wanda, the couple told them not to worry about anything, since the honeymooners would make it just fine at Sergei's apartment. They understood their guests were volunteering for a cause that demanded work here and now. It was a good cause, and Irina was developing a special interest from the standpoint of her own career in international affairs. She wanted to keep an eye on this case and be of service. Being involved, and the possibility of helping in the evolution by purpose case, gave her goosebumps.

Wanda made sure her idea made sense, and knowing that Liz would definitely ask her, conducting a search was essential. By evening, she had confirmed what hit her was not addressed in either *The Origin of Species* or *The Descent of Man*. Having cleared Darwin's books, she proceeded to develop the little plan she had to discuss later with Liz and the coalition at school.

The university pub was built at the very centre of the campus. It looked cool, with a set of stairs going down to the basement where there was a bar and a stage used by students who were serious performers. Bands would come to play there, attracting the crowds. Styles would depend on the day: classical, jazz, rock, or techno-disco were the most popular ones and always drew large audiences. When Wanda arrived, she met Irina and Sergei. They and a small crew were preparing to shoot a video for a pop band, two girls with two guys playing catchy music. Although Wanda did not understand the lyrics, she figured out what the song was about once she saw a huge LCD TV screen on the back wall with the words to the song in English. "That's fantastic", she told her friends.

"You like it, huh?" Irina asked. "They are making that video to promote good and friendly relations, alluding to the Winter Games."

Wanda waited until Liz came to talk about her plan for the photo session with the athletes. But first, Wanda would have to deal with their reactions.

The university pub was crowded that evening. Russians tend to be social creatures who like to exchange things such as gifts, news, and kisses! Kissing very passionately, Irina and Sergei were a fine example. Liz and Wanda gave them some space, so the couple could spend time with each other. The girls mingled

with the band's roadie and friends, learning Russian words, drinking soft drinks with a touch of vodka, and laughing. They talked about the atmosphere as the band started its gig. Outside, it had begun to snow, but the women had that issue sorted; coat-checkers also accepted boots, so female students were able to wear strapped shoes with their fancy dresses. Irina was more casually dressed than many of the others. Being only days away from getting married and two months from graduation, she explained, "As a senior here, I do feel comfortable wearing shorts with stockings and a silk top. Sergei told me he really likes all this."

The coalition group waited for Wanda to disclose her game plan. Once she did, feedback was not so great. Liz protested, "Wanda, are you out of your senses?"

"No, I'm actually quite serious, Liz."

After a moment, Irina intervened. "Liz, you know this shocked me quite a bit at first, but on second thought, it does make sense, however wild or odd it may sound."

Wanda went on to say, "It is about science – biology, anatomy, right? Regardless of people's financial or social status and cultural background, it is something already established in the mindset, ours and theirs. Can't you see? Darwin didn't deal with it, yet it has a lot to do with the rules dictated by him. I mean … natural selection/sexual selection."

Liz began to concede. "And what do you propose?"

"I want the athletes to have two photographs taken … like before and after. I know that's going to deliver a strong punch in the courtroom; one they cannot redirect."

Irina added her voice. "I'd say it's true. So much to beat on in that particular. Plus, the judge happens to be a woman and will understand! I like this, Wanda. You count me in."

Early the next morning, Wanda got really busy. She called all the athletes and tried to persuade them to help. As soon as Wanda shared a few words about her plan, many turned her down due to reasonable concerns, such as their images and whether the photos would become instruments of mockery. A strong negotiator, however, Wanda Newtowne appealed to each of them with a simple, honest approach. "I understand your doubts. This is no ordinary request but one that can certainly bring humankind closer to true science to get it straight once and for all. In a few weeks, you all will have read the conclusion and a decision made here regarding one of the most controversial hot-button topics of all time. So I'm asking for your valuable contribution by means of your pictures."

Irina Baranchuk took it from there and promised each of the girls they would get to meet faculty and friends at her university. There would also be a wonderful reception at the pub afterwards to thank them. The deal was made with the four girls, after discussing a minor change. Instead of two photos of each, it was decided there would only be one taken of the group, posing together in the university theatre. Everybody involved were excited. They would all meet in seven days. The timing was perfect, as the opening ceremony of the Olympics at Sochi would take place three days later.

Irina received a call from Jacob's lawyer to inform her the judge wanted to meet with the parties prior to the hearing to have on record the opening statements for the defendant. He wanted this done during the arraignment, before prosecutors formally charged Jacob Kodnia. The judge wanted the defence to indicate exactly what they were seeking in addition to having all charges dismissed. This partially opened a door for the lawyer, and when the coalition group found out, they decided unanimously to use Darwin's biographical record as evidence in court.

PRELIMINARY HEARING

DEFENCE ATTORNEY VLADIMIR TSERKOV WALKED into the courtroom accompanied by Jacob and the coalition. After a formal greeting, he approached the bench to address the court, presided over by judge Anya Kuziora. The solicitor proceeded to read,

> Mr. Charles Darwin, nineteenth-century biologist, was a student at Edinburgh and matriculated there to study medicine. During his time in Scotland, he decided medicine was not his vocation and moved to Cambridge to study theology at Christ's College. There, he became friends with J. Henslow, a scientifically inclined clergyman and professor of botany. Darwin graduated with a BA in theology, spending a great deal of time discussing faith and science with Henslow and developing his well-known interest in natural science. It was Henslow who secured a place for Darwin on an expedition aboard the *Beagle,* travelling for years during the 1830s.

This portion of Darwin's biography surprised some of the people who were present. It was one example of how media or the authorities do not always seek accurate records. The solicitor continued.

> Darwin began his worldwide expedition following his graduation from Christ's College in 1831. His beloved daughter Anne Elizabeth was born in 1841, but a fatal illness caused the child to die in 1851, at age ten. This tragedy delivered Darwin a blow from which he would not recover. Although he distanced himself from smiling, warm-hearted churchgoers, his belief in a supreme being remained, as it can be verified in his literary works, citing God as the Creator – capital C – having adopted a more objective attitude which rested

chiefly on his observations of nature, namely identifying and classifying plants and lower species of the animal kingdom, such as insects, birds and fish. He also had the misfortune to go through a recurring illness that he contracted while in South America, where he conducted a study on insects native to the area. These insects, the vinchuca, transmitted the Chagas disease that affected Darwin for long periods each year for the rest of his life.

Finally, Vladimir Tserkov said, "Not only should the charges against Jacob Kodnia be dismissed, but on consideration of all the facts involved in this matter, we are requesting freedom in the classrooms to study both evolution and creation, without restrictions imposed by school officials who otherwise may choose to adopt one as the truth, suppressing the other without an opportunity for analysis."

Judge Kuziora acknowledged the statements and said, "The court has granted the petition filed at the time of the arraignment so as to allow for the hearing to be bilingual. To that effect, arrangements have been made for two court reporters to be present. The reason I granted this request is not because, as stated, Mr. Kodnia is fluent in English as well as Russian, but the fact the case is heavily connected to Darwin, who was a British subject, and his works are likely to be cited many times, making it necessary for accurate understanding. Court is adjourned."

THE TRIAL BEGINS

COALITION MEMBERS ENJOYED PARTS OF the month of February, including the athletes' photo session, school pub parties, the Winter Games, and of course, Irina and Sergei's wedding. But then it was time for the group to face a very important situation: the trial. What was at stake was more than a two-year sentence for an elderly, introverted man with a bright mind. Freedom in the classroom and education without chains and whips were also at stake. Historically, science made huge progress when truth prevailed over brainwash indoctrination; observations made, measurements noted, and tests conducted are key procedures in the field of science. Incidentally, exercising faith also requires a mind free of the interference of idols and without acts of violence, such as threats of "Convert now or die," or "Recant or else." Although it could be said faith has a wider spectrum, some beliefs become the basis of laws in many countries. Those laws reflect the basic foundation on which humankind can function. These nations command their citizens to refrain from stealing, killing, lying, committing adultery, and so on.

Jacob Kodnia understood early on that a setback could turn the trial into a platform or catapult. Inside the courtroom, he shared occasional impressions with Vladimir Tserkov. Jacob received an up-to-date report about his supporters, the coalition, who were to be more than passive observers. According to the plan, after the prosecution called its witnesses, Wanda would take the stand to give an account of what happened on the day of the lecture that led to Jacob's arrest. That way, the defence would concentrate on solid ground material instead of wasting time cross-examining individuals who did not understand what evolution by purpose meant.

The prosecution team, consisting of a man and a woman, knew why the case had to go to court. They were satisfied with the EU ban on teaching creationism in schools. Prosecutors Boris Razputin and Valentina Krashmanova believed they could show Jacob was a confused old man, who might be able to walk away with a suspended sentence but without any pull regarding the suppression of creationism.

The first witness to testify was Inspector Trotsky. Without throwing mud on Jacob, Inspector Trotsky related his duty, stating his job demanded actions. Trotsky did not elaborate on how he received the order to take Jacob away, limiting his testimony to stating he was commissioned to pick him up.

At that moment, Liz walked into the courtroom and took a seat near the door to avoid distractions. She decided not to join her group unless a recess was called. Going along with fashion trends, Liz dressed casually that day, sporting a long, thick shirt with the Olympics logo and the inscription "Sochi 2014." It was paired with a miniskirt with white, blue, and red stripes. Long white boots and stockings completed her outfit that made her look like a Moscow girl.

2 Theories

- Common ground
- differences

60k ó 60k

EVOLUTION	CREATION
Life origin: Darwin cites a Creator; Many evolution supporters deny that by answering <unknown>	**Life origin:** God Provision as well as variety of life forms are part of God's plan Physical body temporary. Eternity.
Natural Selection: Responsible for all changes; gradual modifications determine whether a species thrives or is to become extinct. Struggle for survival. Over time, N.S. removes features / things of no use or profit.	**Holy Spirit:** Giver of life, responsible for sustaining life; when the spirit departs from a body, it dies. Sweat and toil, to make a living in a harsh environment
Laws of variation: within species, dominant and recessive traits such as hair & eyes. Crossing species: sterility	**Law:** Do's and don'ts; books of Exodus and Leviticus. Genetics manifests after Noah; descendants evolved establishing ethnic groups.
Sexual Selection: Males' struggle for the possession of females; more appeal, more progeny.	Produce offspring; multiply. No sexual perversion.

Two Theories

- common ground
- differences

Evolution	Creation
Life origin: Darwin cites a Creator. Many evolution supporters deny that by answering, "unknown" Natural selection: Responsible for all changes; gradual modifications determine whether a species thrives or is to become extinct. Struggle for survival. Over time, natural selection removes features/things of no use or profit. Laws of variation; within species dominant and recessive traits, such as hair and eyes. Crossing species: sterility. Sexual selection: Males' struggle for the possession of females; more appeal, more progeny.	Life origin: God. Provision as well as variety of life forms are part of God's plan. Physical body temporary. Eternity. Holy Spirit: Giver of life, responsible for sustaining life; when the spirit departs from a body, it dies. Sweat and toil to make a living in a harsh environment. Law: Dos and do nots; books of Exodus and Leviticus. Genetics manifest after Noah; descendants evolved, establishing ethnic groups. Produce offspring; multiply. No sexual perversion.

Despite Liz's attempt to remain unnoticed, Boris recognised her almost immediately. "You know the girl who just walked in here?" he asked Valentina. "It's Liz McGillan, a witness for Jacob."

Valentina replied, "Yes, but it's that other woman over there – Wanda – near Jacob who is ready to testify."

Boris had an idea. "Let's change this. Let's call Liz. She looks like a dumb blonde without a clue."

A brief argument between legal teams broke out as the defence team struggled to maintain the strategy. Judge Kuziora sided with the prosecutor, citing names of persons willing to come forward to testify. Liz McGillan was among the names registered.

While that was argued, Wanda quickly said to Liz, "No problem, Liz. You've got this. Go and tell them about the lecture … and also about your inspired moment. Remember, the two theories … side by side?" Looking over her shoulder, Liz saw Irina, who nodded in agreement with Wanda. Her doubts vanished instantly as she stood before the judge to be sworn in.

Boris began to question Liz. "How did you come to know Jacob Kodnia?"

"My friend and I were walking when we received an invitation to attend a lecture, Mr. Kodnia's lecture on evolution by purpose. We decided to go."

Boris asked, "Have you ever witnessed any type of lecture about evolution or creation in the past?"

Recalling the incident at Moscow's international airport, Liz answered, "Actually, yes, it was like a riot at the airport, really … chanting some stuff I couldn't interpret. But I read signs they held up that said 'Survival of the Fittest' and that sort of messages."

Boris tried to put some pressure on Liz. "Are you familiar with Darwin's works?"

"Yes I am. They are valuable to me."

"Do you believe in what the Bible teaches?"

"Yes, sir, I do."

Boris Razputin thought he had cornered Liz. Sarcastically he asked, "How is that possible, Ms. McGillan?"

After gaining Judge Kuziora's permission, Liz took a marker and began to write on a board used for exhibits. First she outlined the basics of both theories.

Surprisingly, it appeared the two had a lot in common. Turning to face Judge Kuziora, Liz said, "History shows people used ideas conceived by others to promote a secret agenda. In Darwin's case, certain leaders used evolution as a way to push a sinister political plot that resulted in the murders of millions of persons. Darwin seemed quite mesmerised by observing birds eating insects, but according to his own writings, Darwin was quite disturbed by the actions of some tribes in a remote location from whom he witnessed unspeakable practices, including infanticide."

Attempting to diminish the value of Liz's statement, the prosecutor asked, "So is it infanticide that leads you to believe both concepts are similar in general?" At that, Vladimir Tserkov objected, and Judge Kuziora sided with him, instructing Boris to rephrase the question. So he asked, "What other example can you give us that establishes a strong similarity or bond between evolution and the Bible?"

As Liz began the mental process required to answer the prosecutor's question, she sensed the importance of the unexpected turn of events and how her testimony would help the case. Looking around her, all eyes staring, scanning, watching for clues; the judge, the coalition, and the foes. The more she thought about it, the more energised and excited she felt. Liz felt a sudden warmth and waves of pleasure as she realised she was prepared for this – the revelation of her discovery.

"Well, Miss McGillan?" Boris asked.

"To answer your question, sir, I could give a detailed list of examples. But for the sake of the people here, let me start with one: natural selection, which, by way of definition, is quite comparable to what in the Bible is referred to as Holy Spirit, not a creature, a man, or woman, but an agent that brings things to life, making changes. Yes, we know that term, don't we? It transforms what is created, plants, animals, stars, galaxies. This agent I am referring to, whether from Darwin or the Bible, is the source of life and the one sustaining life, operating in a rather orderly fashion, as if by a code of laws." The adrenaline in Liz's body kept her going.

"Just one question about the last thing you said. This force works under certain rules or laws. Is that right? "How can we tell it is so?" Boris was trying to trap Liz, ushering her to make some contradiction and still hoping to make her look foolish and clueless.

"Three very clear examples prove that point, sir. Darwin wrote that there is an agent similar to natural selection, which he called sexual selection. It is a source of change, with the power to remove features or structures that do not contribute to the success of an individual in leaving progeny. Besides the fact that species cannot cross, sterility principle. Another example would be the periodic table of the elements. If you study chemistry or physics, you know each element has atoms with an identical number of protons in the nucleus. And one more example is the macro cosmos, where stars burn until they run out of fuel. They are always under the force of gravity which, by the way, keeps them spinning in such an orderly manner people can actually predict their movements."

Judge Kuziora was impressed by what she heard so far. She was also amused, having noticed the change of witnesses was not working well for the prosecution team. The judge thought Liz gave prosecutors the wrong impression 'a sexy blonde in a cute outfit with no brain'. Silence in the courtroom prompted Judge Kuziora to ask, "Any more questions for the witness?"

"Uhm, no, Your Honour. That's it for now."

It was now the defence's turn. Vladimir Tserkov asked Liz to tell the court about the lecture, especially how Jacob Kodnia interacted with his audience and how he presented his views on Darwin. Liz made clear that Darwin gave the world a lot of information, accelerating the advent of biology. But Darwin believed he would be proven wrong about some things in the future. "Do you believe there is a link between evolution and Bible in the form of some specific event evolutionary science should consider as proof of this?"

Liz answered, saying,

The story of Noah is recorded in Genesis. A great flood caused by incessant downpour was meant to destroy life. So Noah received instructions to build the ark in which he and his family – wife, three sons, and their wives – along with two of every animal according to its kind – male and female – would be preserved. Chapters 7, 8, and 9 describe the whole ordeal and what happened after the deluge. Chapters 9 and 10 contain the claim that Noah's descendants populated the earth, having gone to distant places, resulting in different nations with their own ethnicity. Since the Scriptures do not attribute the variety of races to magical arts but explain quite clearly that a progressive cycle of life allowed for species to multiply and evolve – with special emphasis on humankind – it is obvious to me, to Jacob Kodnia, and to others that the God of creation, Yahweh or Jehovah, is quite pro-evolution in view of this story.

"Thank you, Miss McGillan. No more questions."

Next to take the oath was Jacob Kodnia. Vladimir called him to explain the chasm, or huge gap, separating humans from monkeys in appearance and as well as the capacity to learn, interact, and communicate with others. Jacob had long studied all this, leading him to some important conclusions. As Vladimir put a chart on the board, Jacob began to explain how a person's progress is evaluated by means of the five main areas of development.

From early childhood, individuals are observed by family members, teachers, and caretakers, so their development can be measured and understood. This applies to all boys and girls, regular or special ed, as their development is directly linked to five areas.

- speech/language skills (receptive and expressive)
- social skills
- self-help skills
- cognitive (knowledge acquired through perception, reasoning or intuition)
- motor skills (gross and fine motor)

I'll give you an example to prove how these areas are connected and work together. Suppose two friends are in class. One of the two tells the other he has a new book, and his friend asks to see it (speech and social skills). Making sure their hands are clean, the pair sits down to check out the new book (self-help). Paying attention to the book's format, the two kids learn through illustrations (visual) and by reading paragraphs while sharing impressions (auditory stimuli). Thus their cognition skills absorb and retain new information. One of the two kids holds the book as the other makes a drawing of the book's cover (gross and fine motor skills, respectively).

Jacob went on to relate it to Darwin and his findings.

These same skills are substantially different in the development of apes. Darwin wrote about an experiment conducted on monkeys to study behaviour traits. They were given alcoholic drinks, and sure enough, they got drunk. Comical as it must have been, the test pointed out that when monkeys were offered more alcohol the next day, they refused to drink it, possibly because of the hangover they suffered from their previous experience with alcohol. Self-help skills prompted their choice not to mess with liquor. In comparison, we can say that monkeys may have advanced self-help skills regarding things that could harm them, although self-help skills are more than, "drink this, don't drink that." They consist of layers of encoded information that regulate how they conduct themselves. This last point was also verified by Darwin when he mentioned, by way of inferences, that the early progenitors of humankind would have been subject to popularity or shame according to their actions. As far as the other areas, monkeys possess gross motor skills but lack fine motor ones. Speech, an important area, is non-existent.

Social skills may be fairly well established, but cognition is another area that shows huge deficiencies. Learning is a complex function in the brain that makes it possible for an individual to gain knowledge. In order to give a simple to understand analogy, consider two computers. One is brand new, with great capacity in its memory banks, known as read only memory and random access memory. Such capacity makes it possible for the computer to operate efficiently in many tasks. The other computer, being old and primitive, is quite limited in what it can do, because its memory banks are far less advanced. To put it now in natural terms, monkeys are like the other animals: creatures that primarily function within their instincts. Here's what makes humans so different from the other creatures. Humankind relies less on instincts and more on upbringing. This is why we all go to school and spend so much time learning. Besides this academic gap, humankind is far superior to all other animals in the ability to communicate with others –whether concrete or abstract ideas. People are capable of sharing experiences taken from real life as well as dreams and ideas resulting from pure imagination. We have the ability to create things; animals do not. Even children with developmental challenges are capable of sharing thoughts with others and talk about past, present, or future events. Animals can't do that because they lack the capacity to function in those areas.

To conclude, I have to stress that the most advanced monkey is far, far inferior, in comparison, even to a toddler.

With a broad smile on his face, Vladimir uttered, "Thank you, Mr. Kodnia, for your testimony. I'm glad you cleared up a difficult concept for us."

Judge Kuziora asked prosecutors, "Cross-examine?"

Valentina held her hand up and said "Yes, Your Honour." Turning to Jacob, Valentina asked, "So we are unique in that we need to be instructed, compared to all other animals … which kind of have it 'built in', so to speak?"

"Basically yes. In that sense, our infants are really more vulnerable, fragile. Consequently, the character each of us can be remembered by in adulthood does not come straight from birth. It is gradually formed by a series of important events which profoundly impact certain aspects linked to our personality, in conjunction with our natural makeup and aptitudes. It's like two lines interweaving and moulding our character: one being what we are given by natural selection and the other, all relevant experiences – good and bad ones – forming impressions which would have a lifelong effect concerning our perception of life in general as well as on our demeanour. This is why it is such a serious crime to put a child through a traumatic experience. There is no telling how big the risk of damage would be in that young mind afterwards."

Valentina understood quite well what she heard from Jacob, but because she wanted to put Jacob on the spot, she sought a confirmation of statements from him. "So you mean we get to be who we are by some combination of natural traits and whatever we absorb during our years of formation."

"Correct."

"Well then, how would you explain the fact that so many people are victimised by others … assault, abuse, battery, murder?"

"Excuse me, do you want me to answer that based on the survival of the fittest belief or based on what I have discovered?"

After a moment of silence, Valentina replied, "Only your personal thoughts, please."

"All right. Going through a bad experience does not guarantee the victim will later default to it and put someone else through a similar evil. Many times the victim is completely healed in that he or she will make sure others do not go through the same. For example, a parent abandons child, and as an adult, that child becomes a remarkable parent. Unfortunately, though, there are other cases where someone with some unresolved issue due to negative experiences deliberately puts an innocent person through a similar plight … opposite reactions."

"Is there some kind of remedy to stop the propagation of such mental poisoning?"

"Yes, as a matter of fact, it is written, and briefly stated in a few lines."

"You mean the Ten Commandments."

"Precisely. But even for those who reject that type of self-examination, there is for instance, the wisdom of Gandhi, who said something quite in line with that by telling people they must be the change they want to see in the world."

Valentina turned to the judge and said, "No more questions for now."

As Jacob Kodnia stepped down, Vladimir brought a poster made by Jacob and presented it to the court as an exhibit. The poster was a drawing in realistic style, with a monkey on the left side, a question mark in the centre, and a female figure on the right. Once he pinned it to the exhibit board, Vladimir said,

This is a true representation of the problem with the theory that claims we come from monkeys. I am asking the court and everyone here to try to imagine how humankind come from an ape and have two sets of hands, a very different set of bones, including the ribcage, spine, and skull, be covered in fur, incapable of speaking, reading or writing, and all the other shortcomings already mentioned by the defendant. How would it be possible to go from that ape to this girl, with her soft skin; curves; thin hair instead of fur; a nose that is so graceful thanks to a special tiny bridge; a natural capacity to talk, to learn and teach, to share, to create, to worship; and a heart equipped with love for strangers by means of respect and hospitality … love for those who are close to her and count on her in good times and rough times … and love for the man in her life who shares the bed with her? Think about it. Perhaps it won't be such an outrageous thing to realise that the difference between these two is astronomical.

With that, the day in court came to an end. The trial was to continue in seven days. Although there were no comments in the courtroom, the defence made progress, and the coalition felt happy with the way things turned out.

For the prosecution, a new strategy would be needed. Valentina and Razputin spent time analysing the testimony on record and deciding how to prepare for the next court date. They already knew that Wanda Newtowne would be called to testify, and though they imagined she would be capable of going to court with a clear idea of what to say, prosecutors would set up a roadblock so difficult to overcome it might even spell out victory. Valentina and Razputin laughed as they let their imaginations fly.

The coalition went to a restaurant late that night. To their surprise, they were cheered by a clique as they entered. When one of the Russians showed Liz and Wanda a copy of the poster used as evidence in court – the one with the ape and the girl – everybody rejoiced. "Word travels in this town," the coalition commented.

A supporter replied, "Oh, not just the word. We love art, and the poster is really fantastic! We are sick of rubbish being thrown at people as art. Now this is art. Besides, for ages we had pictures of an ape and some weird blend of monkey and man that was partially covered with fur and had front teeth like some kind of wolf. Preposterous and an insult to true science!"

In the back of the restaurant was a pool table. The coalition and the newfound supporters shot some pool as they celebrated the progress. The man who spoke first about the poster also gave the coalition an interesting clue about *The Descent of Man*. Once they heard about it, the group vowed to use it in court. With so many good things happening, it seemed only natural to have a great time.

Science or Mythology?
By Jacob Kodnia

THE TRIAL CONTINUES

Jacob Kodnia's case began to gain attention from average people and the scientific community alike. Although officials did their best to keep it in the dark, courthouse hallways were not exactly airtight, especially when the matter would not be decided in one day. Small groups would stop at the magistrate building, trying to get information about a classic debate on evolution or creation.

Everything was up for review. The prosecution and the defence were determined to show evidence theirs was the correct approach. And though Jacob remained under house arrest – not allowed to meet anybody other than his counsel – he was, in his conversations with Vladimir Tserkov, optimistic about what was happening. Jacob felt grateful for the support from the coalition group, particularly to Liz and Wanda, whom he considered very special young women. He was also grateful to Irina for being so quick to find him a voice in the complicated legal system, which often allows dirt to contaminate the wells of justice.

The poster of the chimp and the girl was quite popular already; it was found on the walls of pubs, school cafeterias, and news boards in churches. A full-size version was even spotted on an underground train, Though its placement was unauthorised, the transport company did not remove it, because publicity resulted in more riders out to get a glimpse of the increasingly popular design. For most people, this was only an invitation to ponder if humankind is related to apes. The difference here was that instead of the picture of a monkey and some wacky humanoid never in existence, there was a picture of the monkey next to a girl who, for all purposes, fit the description of Cleopatra, Queen of Sheba, Ashley Wagner, or Miley Cyrus.

Boris Razputin and Valentina Krashmanova recruited help from a philosopher, humanist, and author they flew in from France. Jean Truefault, also an atheist, sought to promote liberty by the notion, "If it makes you happy, go for it." The coalition did not know about him, but they did not object when his name was added to the witness list. The prosecution team called its witness, and after being sworn in, he proceeded to testify.

"Mr. Truefault, would you tell us about your new book on liberation?"

In response to Valentina's request, he answered, "My book explains the process involved in becoming free from the burden of fear. I tell people to be free, without being frightened by the idea that a Creator will someday judge them for their acts and choices in this life."

"And that's something you actually went through, right?"

"Yes. I was raised by Christians. As I grew up, I began to question some things, to challenge the teachings that come from believing in God."

"What happened then?"

"I felt different. An enormous weight lifted off me as I embraced atheism. Think of it this way. No God above … no fear of impending punishment – you know, spending eternity in hell. No fear of what death could bring. Death takes away all fear, because it is total nothingness and so, fear of a non-existent object. Death is simply a reality to get used to, something to be taken in stride."

On cross-examination, Vladimir asked Jean Truefault how people like himself should cope with the loss of a loved one. The answer was, "Memories create a serene state of mind, a feeling of joy from having known that person."

"That's it?"

"Yes. Life's rituals are unavoidable. For example, going to a funeral to remember a deceased person is a ritual. The one who died lives on through the memories of living individuals."

Vladimir blasted that response. "As you may know, history shows that a number of people do not measure up to be remembered in a neat way. Incidentally, people who would not accept the authority of God. Would you agree, or do you want me to offer names?"

"No need, sir. I get the meaning. Some leave behind a trail of misery and shame."

"Thank you for your understanding. Now I will ask you one thing that I cannot help to wonder about when an atheist speaks. Have you personally searched for him … for the Supreme Being out there in the universe as immeasurably vast as it is?"

"No, I did not."

"Do you … I have to ask you something, but I'll do so by giving you a parable. Two brothers have a conversation; one is a believer, and the other is not. The first says to his brother, 'If not for many other reasons, you should contemplate the belief in the existence of God by this fact: if you are right you are not going to be able to tell me I told you so. And if I am right, you will regret not having paid attention to my warning. And facing the second death, you'd no longer have the power to change your future.' Do you ever wonder what-if?"

"It would be a very serious concern. Your parable reflects that as a nothing to gain but everything to lose prospect for those who don't believe. And it makes some sense. But as for me, I just don't have that on my mind. I don't see the point."

"One last question, Mr. Truefault. People who are blind from birth do not see the world the way we can. They have no idea what a rainbow looks like and have no perception of the difference between green, red, blue, or brown. Actually, they do not know what is dark or light. Still, they do not question anybody about it and have no doubts on whether colours exist. Just because they cannot see them, it does not mean they do not accept the existence of light waves. What do you think in this regard?"

"I never thought about anything like that."

"Thank you, Your Honour. No more questions."

Wanda Newtowne was called as the next witness. Being less than impressed with Truefault's testimony, prosecutors needed to crush Wanda's to control the situation. At Vladimir's request, Wanda explained her involvement in this case by means of a series of events, combined with personal interests.

"Liz McGillan and I have been best friends since childhood. We shared experiences like school crushes, boyfriend dramas, and music preferences. We also have a certain inclination towards intricate issues of life, and we like to get to the bottom of things by digging out as much as possible about those issues or topics. One such thing is the extinction of the dinosaurs, which is connected to another event long ago, the breakup of a gigantic landmass into continents."

Razputin objected on the grounds of lack of relevance. But Judge Kuziora overruled, indicating the fact this earth science enigma was manipulated, resulting in a version of the event that defies all common sense, and was being imposed on students everywhere, much like the theory of evolution.

Wanda continued her testimony.

All schools teach that dinosaurs became extinct as a result of a meteorite hitting the planet. As for the formation of continents, it is taught that Antarctica, South America, India, and Australia were part of a single mass. One day, India began to move from near the South Pole to the Northern Hemisphere, as if it was a surfing board on a beach, forming the Himalayas. They also teach that as if by magic, North America touched South America, and both became glued at the narrow portion of Central America. The truth is, according to the evidence, that the dinosaurs died in massive numbers as a result of a rather abrupt event: the formation of continents. It was like Krakatoa, but much greater in proportion. For this reason, countless dinosaurs were buried alive, resulting in huge deposits of oil, so important to us. As for the continents, India was never near South America, and the mountain range surrounding it was formed in a way similar to the Andes. And Australia broke off from between eastern Africa and India, while the Americas have never been apart.

It is similar to the universe and its origins. Students are obligated to accept the notion that out of nothing came everything, with a bang. However, not one of its proponents – who are in control of textbooks – can explain how it is the universe has no walls. Their own example of the balloon universe proves them wrong. A balloon can inflate as long as the environment that contains it permits. But what can possibly contain this never-ending, open space universe?

Vladimir Tserkov brought her back to the issue on trial. "Why are you here today?"

"We are here to show that neither Mr. Kodnia's works nor his actions justify his current status. We gathered before this court to rectify his case as well as problems arising from unfair restrictions that have been interfering with the education system on a global scale. By this I mean the prohibition to teach evolution in schools, such was the case in 1925 in Tennessee, USA, referred to as the Scopes Monkey Trial. Then we have many places where the opposite idea rules, and the theory of ID is banned. Either way, it is wrong to impede the normal desire to investigate and discover, since science and technology require this sort of work in order to advance. In addition, there is enough evidence to assert that the Scriptures are a solid source of knowledge which civilised people can refer to in building productive lives that, in turn, result in a better society."

"So you are in favour of allowing students to learn both theories, right?"

"Yes, sir."

"Have you read *The Descent of Man*, Ms. Newtowne?"

"Yes, I have."

"What is your opinion?"

Wanda delineated her points.

Darwin consulted with many people, citing their views shared with him; I would by all means recommend *The Descent of Man* to students entering secondary school. However, in my opinion, there are conclusions drawn I believe should belong in one of the following categories.

1. Completely accurate. For example, in describing the process of adaptation, as it is the case with certain birds that underwent a modification of the beak so that they were able to reach deep into a flower to get the nectar. Birds of the same species that do not feed on those flowers have retained the shorter beak.

2. Fairly accurate in consideration of ambiguity. For example, in describing ancient forms of organisation among members of tribes, whom Darwin credited with possessing moral and social qualities, something he believed happened at a very early period with the progenitors of humankind. He also stated that apes are given to imitation, not really to moral values. A better example is Darwin's analysis of the intellectual capacity of man compared to woman. In this respect, he

did make clear that man is by nature more of an achiever: "man attaining to a higher eminence in whatever he takes up than woman can attain." Darwin considered that under the same rigours of early training and instruction, woman could be able to expand her mental capacity. It is known from ancient times and from all over the world that man would carry the responsibilities by means of some physical strength and decision making – especially during times of war – delegating to woman the chores and upbringing of the children. Changes in this traditional way of thinking took place only in recent history. Today's society recognises the skills and high capacity of both sexes, throwing out the idea that one is inferior.

3. Absolute speculation. Certain assumptions made by Darwin failed the test of time at all levels of verification. For example, that our ancestors had a tail and that in those days, both male and female were able to nurse their infants.

Vladimir knew it was time to elaborate on the female side of humankind. "As a woman and based on his works, do you believe Darwin had poor knowledge of the development of a girl into a woman?"

"Yes, sir, I do."

A large television screen was brought into the courtroom and placed between Judge Kuziora and Wanda. Vladimir connected the TV to a computer as Wanda began to explain. "You are about to see an important piece of evidence, something Darwin could never have imagined regarding the feminine side." A live performance of "Somebody to Love" by Justin Bieber was played. It showed a staggering number of girls, ages ranging from about eight to definitely adult, from all ethnic groups imaginable, living in cities like Toronto or New York. Playing back other bits of the documentary allowed Wanda to stress the equality of the sexes, in that girls of different backgrounds were in a state of ecstasy getting to meet the boy of their fancy. She noted that girls do compete for any boy they feel attracted to.

Vladimir Tserkov asked her, "That which you just told this court as the video went on is a point Darwin missed?"

"Yes, it is … in spite of the fact there are historical records describing what I am testifying now."

"Can you name those records, please?"

"Yes, a number of them, actually, starting with the book of Esther. She was a girl in a foreign land who had a long preparation. Esther and many other girls were selected to compete for the chance to become the king's wife in that land. They all had to endure treatments to maximize their beauty, while at the same time, it would help them mentally. After their period of preparation, the king would find a young woman from among them he could love for her beauty, sensuality, and personality. It took twelve months, and Esther was chosen, becoming queen."

"Do you want to add more historical references, Miss Newtowne?"

"Yes, sir. Another important source is the Song of Solomon, which is really captivating by virtue of the style and meaning. A man and a woman, deeply in love, exchange expressions of endearment and compliments in the highest order through poetry. The narrative throughout this short book is loaded with hot references that indicate a very intense sexual craving." Wanda read a few passages to make her illustration clear.

> Like an apple tree among the trees of the forest, so is my dear one among the sons. His shade I have passionately desired and there I have sat down, his fruit has been sweet to my palate. He brought me into the house of wine and his banner over me was love … sustain me with apples for I am lovesick … my dear one is mine and I am his … on my bed during the nights I have sought the one whom my soul has loved.

"With those words, recorded in chapters 2 and 3, the girl pours out her love for him. He responds with his expressions about what sets her apart from all others, including queens and concubines –whom he had – and his declaration of love gives a description of this girl, 'blameless one … without defect.' The first eight verses in chapter 7 do tell us about it.

How beautiful your steps have become in your sandals … the curving of your thighs are like ornaments, the work of an artisan's hands. Your navel roll is a round bowl. Let not the mixed wine be lacking from it. Your belly is a heap of wheat fenced with lilies. Your two breasts are like two young ones the twins of a female gazelle. Your neck is like an ivory tower. Your eyes are like the pools in Heshbon. Your nose is like the tower of Lebanon. Your head is like Carmel and the tresses of your head like reddish-purple wool. The king is held bound by the flowings. How beautiful you are, how pleasant you are, oh beloved girl, among exquisite delights. The stature of yours does resemble a palm tree and your breasts date clusters; I have said, "I shall climb the palm tree that I may take hold of its fruits, and please, may your breasts become clusters of the wine and the fragrance of your nose like apples and your palate like the best wine."

Wanda finished her reading. The courtroom was silent for a few seconds, until someone by the entrance said, "My oh my … lovey-dovey paperbacks have nothing on this one, baby!" People burst into laughter. Judge Kuziora raised a hand to get everyone quiet again. Vladimir approached the bench but then took a couple of steps towards Wanda, he asked, "Do you wish to add anything else?"

"Just one more point. According to Genesis 3, God himself spoke following Adam and Eve's failure, informing them concerning Eve that 'Your craving will be for your husband,' which is a command that remains down to this day, as we see young girls deeply connected to the need for their acceptance and praise from boys. They feel the need to catch their attention, motivating them to look their best and act like the coolest. In comparison, boys generally need more time to become mature enough to perceive … to notice … a girl's personal interest."

"Thank you, Ms. Newtone."

Judge Kuziora turned to the prosecution team, who had by then verified the Bible quotes made by Wanda. Boris Razputin saw an opportunity to tear down what Wanda was building – trust. "You believe girls grow up before boys the same age?"

"In most cases, girls show the early signs of maturity before boys do."

"And you attribute that characteristic … that gender trait … to Genesis 3?"

"Yes, sir."

Razputin had a copy of the European Union's Constitution, plus a copy of the recent resolution banning the teaching of creationism from schools. Showing both documents to Wanda, he said, "It seems the Bible has no problems with relationships based on a steady, permanent bond. But there is, however, a type of relationship that won't stand the chance, regardless of how committed partners may be. I'm referring to gay individuals. Do you agree?"

"Yes."

"Why would the 'God of love' oppose and even punish those engaging in gay relationships?"

"Do you really care to know?"

"Oh, absolutely."

"Well, the normal cycle of life includes courtship and intercourse, but these are to obey laws of nature, observing rules. Naturally, a male and a female comfort each other with the use of their bodies. Then they become parents and build a family, and resulting from that a community and a country."

"Are you aware gay people are recognised and allowed to live with someone of their own sex in today's world?"

"Yes, I am. Still they live outside the will of God in doing so."

"Please explain."

"We are equipped with a mental function telling right and wrong according to the choices we make. Homosexuals invariably suffer a great deal, struggling with some inclination they know to be wrong. And the reason they go through all that difficulty is that it involves a complete transformation of themselves, which removes traces of their personality, to be replaced with others. God has a purpose for us all. If we fall under addictions and vices, though, we change for worse the blessings that await us. When a person turns to homosexuality, he or she acts under a distorted state of mind that causes trouble by using the body in a destructive way."

"You just said the words 'distorted' and 'destructive'. What tells you it is so?"

"As a social worker, I know from experience that homosexuals have an element of psychological chaos resulting from bad experiences during childhood: molestation, physical abuse, and so on. Verbal assault is another cause, perpetrated by bullies in the home or at school, who would pick on a kid with a vulnerable mind, until the aggression strips that kid from his confidence and dignity. A mental state of confusion may lead from there to hearing from gay adults who tend to present same-sex romance as a cool alternative, promising happiness after the struggle.

"Are you not being a bit harsh on those who seek a romantic involvement with people of their own sex?"

"It depends on how you analyse this matter, really. I am in no way condemning them; I have no interest and no authority. But the more I've learned about them, the more I can link this to some form of addiction, not far from the one who seeks a needle, who in truth is victimised, transforming his or her mind, and does not consider the cost of the next fix. The person with such an addiction experiences a great deal of pain or anxiety. The distorted mind also leads to neglect of the proper care of the body."

"You sound narrow-minded, Miss Newtowne."

"So far I've tried to explain this sensitive issue in a diplomatic way. Let me add, however, a quick statement just to be clear. When a male lies with another male, one of them treats the other like a female, and that one has to pretend to be a female. But because the pair does not have organs that physically complement, they are forced to exchange natural sexual relations for unnatural ones to express themselves. While I find this repulsive and disgusting, I do feel some degree of pity for those accepting a lie."

"Is that why God sent angels to destroy Sodom-Gomorrah, as stated in Genesis 19?"

"There was not only sexual perversion in that area but excessive pride, which made people rather violent. Sexual practices of any kind can be propagated as rapidly as a case of flu. But there was no sign of remorse nor the desire to get away from it. Except for Lot's household."

"Speaking of them," Razputin quickly commented, thinking he finally trapped her, "I never heard any preacher or Bible reader ever mention the latter part of Genesis 19. You know, the part in which Lot's daughters take turns with him. What do you say?"

"I think you would understand if you cared to read it attentively, from verses 30 to 38. Sulphur and fire rained down, destroying the cities completely. Everyone died; even Lot's wife perished. So it was just Lot and his two daughters. It shouldn't be hard to imagine that what they experienced was quite like the end of the world, leaving the girls in a clear, understandable state of shock. This can easily affect the ability to think straight. Notice that Lot was under the influence of narcotics, and the girls had no malice in their way of thinking, only sheer fear and concern for being left as sole survivors. That's why it is written that one of the girls said to the other, 'There is no man in the land to have relations,' so as to continue the process of life – babies born – to start the cycle over. I dare to say they had a panic attack caused by the incredible devastation they witnessed. This was followed by uncertainty … not a perverted fantasy."

As Wanda stood to head down the steps, she motioned to Vladimir. They asked Judge Kuziora to admit a photograph of herself and Liz McGillan, taken while they were in secondary school, one afternoon at the beach. The photograph was a reaction to a lesson given in biology class that day, when the teacher tried to force into the girls' minds the idea they came from apes. Because of this, Liz and Wanda went to the beach, each wearing a small but flattering bikini. Seeing their reflection in a mirror, both of them said, "Darwin misunderstood," implying he was misunderstood and that he was mistaken as well about the apes. They added, "Monkey resemblance? We don't see it," and discarded the picture of a chimp and the orang the teacher gave them in class. The court admitted the girls' picture and the two documents from Razputin, dismissing everybody afterwards.

The defence felt optimistic, calling this difficult hearing positive. The coalition decided the next court date would be for Irina to testify. She told her friends she was willing to speak about something she had discovered in her married life. She also volunteered to explain the photo shoot taken at her school with the four athletes. Since she really wanted to step up as a witness, Liz and Wanda felt good about the plan. Vladimir also told them Jacob would be asked to testify one more time about what he believed might be a breakthrough, alluding to the problem evolutionists have with the question of how life began. It had been another exciting day for the group.

To their surprise, the coalition continued to gain support from many in Moscow. After being spotted just outside the Church of the Archangel Michael, near the Kremlin, they were asked about the case. "We are doing what we can," members of the group replied. The people on the street who approached the coalition wanted answers. They wanted the truth. Liz, Wanda, and Irina told them to hang on for a few more days and asked them to pray for a positive outcome, which most likely would have an impact on future generations. "today's decisions affect how people will live."

The three friends went to meet Sergei, who had been busy working. "He has been very helpful," Irina told Liz and Wanda about her husband.

"I'll bet!!" Liz said in reply with a giggle.

"Really, I mean helpful to the case," Irina said, decidedly amused. Then she asked the two, "I know that neither of you are in a serious romantic relationship right now, but have you had a long, steady one in the past?"

Wanda answered first, saying, "I've had a few short-lived relationships. The most significant one was dating Lizzy's cousin, Nick McGillan."

"What about you, Liz?" Irina enquired, having noticed Wanda needed privacy.

"I kept a long relationship with a boy who was our classmate. It was cool in a way and goofy in another. But the time came when I couldn't promise to be his-and-his every day, from night 'til morning, because of my own workload – my mission – so he understood. Presently, I am involved with a singer who is determined to fight head-on some of the poverty in the world. His music is a platform for a cause."

"Fantastic, Liz. I can see you all will be able to understand what I am going to testify … even if you haven't had the experience in its full context. By the way, after this is over, it may be time for the pair of you to consider where you want to be and how you want to live. Maybe, just maybe, it would be about time for new horizons." Irina's words left Liz and Wanda thinking. Then, Irina explained what she had in mind for her day in court.

CREATION or EVOLUTION ?

Darwin misunderstood... monkey resemblance ?

We don't see it

darwinwentwrong   #nomonkeyinus

IRINA'S TURN

WAKING UP THAT PRISTINE SPRING morning had a special effect on Irina. Her beloved had just left their home but not before exchanging expressions of love. *We can't get enough of each other,* she thought. Looking out the window, she could see far in the distance chunks of ice already melting on the waters of the Moscova, the river that runs through the city.

A while later, she met the coalition group in the lobby of the courthouse, ready to deal with the rest of the legal process. Prosecutors had a witness who stated he left the place where Jacob gave his lecture feeling worried and disturbed, although he could not directly blame Jacob for it. He admitted the controversy, and particularly a possible reaction from officials made him uncomfortable in view of politics. Irina waited until her name was called.

"Irina Liubovna Baranchuk," the clerk called.

"Right here" she answered in Russian, taking quick steps towards the judge in order to be sworn in. She promised to declare the truth as best as she knew how. Irina related to the court her experience at school, her job prospects, and her firm decision to work for the common good rather than endorse more violence. The latter was in clear reference to what her country went through during the past century. Vladimir knew the cue for action – the real evidence she intended to offer – would come on cross-examination, after saying she had her own evidence to make her believe Jacob Kodnia was not wrong in his observations.

The solicitor asked, "Would you elaborate on your statement? You indicated you have evidence of your own basically corroborating what Mr. Kodnia theorised."

"Yes. My husband, Sergei, and I got married last month. We had been dating for a while, but we … uh, we did not experiment a whole lot." For first time, Irina felt a bit nervous.

Razputin put some pressure. "Can you be more specific, please?"

"All right. What I mean to say is that I never imagined there are so many ways to exchange love. He and I … well, we used to have a little intimacy, but now we have explored more and more ways of loving each other, about a hundred different ways, positions, things to do. It is quite fascinating, really. And I have to tell you, humankind cannot be compared to the other species of the animal kingdom. No, not even in this aspect. Minding the fact we are shaped by how we grow up, not so much by instincts – like all animals do – it is amazing that man and woman have at their disposal so many ways to experience pleasure as they truly give themselves to each other, sharing loads of things with waves of pleasure that leave no shame when they realise they have become one family. This type of union is what the Scriptures tell us of—"

"What about gay couples, then?"

"I'm afraid they have been deceived, missing out so much that does not even require a brainwashing to accept themselves and later to be accepted by others. All that weird stuff they need digested to reprogram the brain like that, and at the end, they are fooling themselves. Let's bear in mind animals are what Darwin studied so well. It is interesting to study Darwin. I did read his works, and I admit I admire his hard work as well as his narrations, how he explained his views. One great point here is that we learn from Darwin not only by what he described and said but by what he never said."

"Exactly what do you mean, Mrs. Baranchuk?"

"I just told you that man and woman have many ways of loving. Animals don't; they are stuck in a one-track situation. Homosexuality robs its victims of the real joy we are meant to experience with the right person. Now, regarding Darwin, you should be able to tell us if he ever mentioned homosexuality or that lifestyle. No, he remained absolutely silent on the subject."

Boris Razputin began to sweat profusely. Attempting to rush her, he asked Irina, "There's no mention of homosexuality at all?"

"Go figure. There is one passage concerning ancient Greece. Darwin wrote, 'The Greeks may have retrograded from a want of coherence between the many small states, from the small size of their whole country, from the practice of slavery, or from extreme sensuality, for they did not succumb until they were enervated and corrupt to the very core.' And there's something else we should observe: what animals – what species – practice homosexuality? Do any birds, fish, or horses? What animal freely choose that lifestyle?" There was complete silence in the courtroom. "It appears Mr. Kodnia was right. It's all in the mind. In great measure, we become who we are based on what our brain is fed with. Good stuff and bad stuff will make a mark inside. Jesus put it correctly, saying that what we feed our minds with will be apparent in what we say: good thinking, good conversation, nasty thinking, nasty vocabulary. It couldn't be more clear."

Razputin asked the court for a recess and was granted two hours. When court reconvened, the solicitor changed the subject. He asked Irina about a broken rule that could be indicative of an error in the way natural selection-sexual selection worked. It was then that Vladimir brought the photograph taken at the university with the four girls from the Olympics, and the very distinctive feature of that photograph was that all four girls showed body hair. Each girl had removed body hair on only half her body, leaving the other half with plenty of unwanted hair on the armpit and leg. They saw their different ethnicities as an opportunity for a joke, sticking on their belly a tag: Miss Middle East, Miss Africa, Miss Europe, and Miss Far East. Irina explained the purpose of the photograph.

According to Charles Darwin, the struggle between males for
the possession of the females is decided by sexual selection;
being more vigorous or having special features will make some
males more appealing, and they would leave most progeny.

These four athletes shaved one side of the body to show something that always had repercussions. Regardless of race and background, girls do not want certain hair to grow. They are aware of what it does to their looks, and they don't want it. Darwin stated that by natural selection, and even more so by sexual selection, features on the body that do not aid in the process of bringing offspring because of not having any use, or because it would make them less appealing would be removed and eliminated so descendents were spared from such inconvenience or defect. Minding Darwin's rules on how the selection process works, we have a problem here, because this annoying feature every girl has to take care of certainly would have been gone by now. Reality, though, proves the genetic information found in each of us remains unaffected, and all that good-for-nothing body hair grows back, giving females all over the world a serious aggravation. In case someone thinks this is blown out of proportion, let's look at a famous singer who, in her free time, offers advice to pre-teenage girls on how to get rid of body hair. Girls aged eleven and twelve talk with their classmates about what each does to remove that hair. This should really prove my point. Hair removal is a powerful, solid business worldwide, but based on Darwin, becoming divested of hair was natural for us. So what happened? I mean, how come that hair grows under the arms and down the legs?"

Irina raised her hand for Vladimir to see, and another document emerged. This one was from the USSR's 1952 archives. Three illustrations published in early editions of Darwin's *The Descent of Man* were edited out since then. On close examination, it was clear why. The embryo of a dog was next to one of a human. The drawings were made using shading that made both look similar, thereby overthrowing the notion of complexity separating them.

Judge Kuziora had to shout to restore order in the courtroom. It was too much. Not only was humankind somewhat more advanced than monkeys, the gestation process of a baby was now likened to that of a dog. Judge Kuziora was increasingly displeased with the trial, but this last issue upset her. She dismissed the parties and ordered Jacob Kodnia to testify one more time by the end of the week. "April third," she noted. After those words, Judge Kuziora left the courtroom.

ILLUSTRATIONS FOUND IN EARLY EDITIONS OF THE DESCENT OF MAN, LATER EDITED OUT

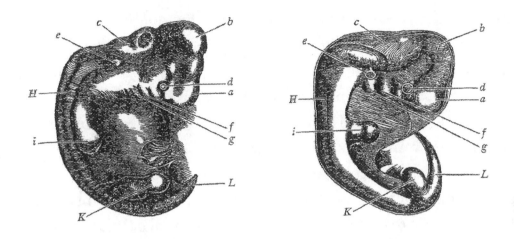

Fig. 1 Upper figure human embryo, from Ecker. Lower figure that of a dog, from Bischoff.

a. Forebrain, cerebral hemispheres, etc.; *b*. Mid-brain, corpora quadrigemina; *c*. Hindbrain, cerebellum, medula oblongata; *d*. Eye; *e*. Ear; *f*. First visceral arch; *g*. Second visceral arch; *H*. Vertebral

Embryonic Development. The human is developed from an ovule, about the 125th of an inch in diameter, which differs in no respect from the ovules of other animals. The embryo itself at a very early period can hardly be distinguished from that of other members of the vertebrate kingdom. At this period, the arteries run in arch-like branches, as if to carry the blood to branchiæ which are not present in the higher vertebrata, though the slits on the sides of the neck still remain (*f*, *g*, fig. 1), marking their former position. At a somewhat later period, when the extremities are developed, "the feet of lizards and mammals," as the illustrious von Baer remarks, "the wings and feet of birds, no less than the hands and feet of man, all arise from the same fundamental form." It is, says Professor Huxley,[1]

---
1 *Man's Place in Nature*, 1863, p. 67.

"quite in the later stages of development that the young human being presents marked differences from the young ape, while the latter departs as much from the dog in its developments, as the man does. Startling as this last assertion may appear to be, it is demonstrably true."

As some of my readers may never have seen a drawing of an embryo, I have given one of man and another of a dog at about the same early stage of development, carefully copied from two works of undoubted accuracy.[2]

In many monkeys, which do not stand high in the order, as baboons and some species of *Macacus*,[3] the upper portion of the ear is slightly pointed, and the margin is not at all folded inwards. But if the margin were to be thus folded, a slight point would necessarily project inwards towards the centre, and probably a little outwards from the plane of the ear; and this I believe to be their origin in many cases. On the other hand, Professor L. Meyer, in an able paper recently published,[4] maintains that the whole case is one of mere variability: and that the projections are not real ones, but are due to the internal cartilage on each side of

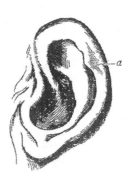

Fig. 2 Human Ear, modelled and drawn by Mr. Woolner.

a. The projecting point.

---

2   The human embryo (upper fig.) is from Ecker, *Icones Phys.*, 1851–1859, tab. xxx, fig. 2. This embryo was ten lines in length, so the drawing is much magnified. The embryo of the dog is from Bischoff, *Entwicklungsgeschichte des Hunde-Eies*, 1845, tab. xi, fig. 42 в. This drawing is five times magnified, the embryo being twenty-five days old. The internal viscera have been omitted, and the uterine appendages in both drawings removed. I was directed to these figures by Professor Huxley, from whose, *Man's Place in Nature,* the idea of giving them was taken. Haeckel has also given analogous drawings in his *Schöpfungsgeschichte.*

3   See also some remarks and the drawings of the ears of the Lemuroidea in Messrs. Murie and Mivart's excellent paper in *Transactions of the Zoological Society*, vii (1869), 6, 90.

4   "Über das Darwin'sche Spitzohr," *Archiv für ???*

the points not having been fully developed. I am quite ready to admit that this is the correct explanation in many instances as in those figured by Professor Meyer, in which there are several minute points, or the whole margin is sinuous. I have myself seen, through the kindness of Dr. L. Down, the ear of a microephalousidiot, on which there is a projection on the outside of the helix, and not on the inward folded edge, so this point can have no relation to a former apex of the ear. Nevertheless in some cases, my original view that the points are vestiges of the tips of formerly erect and pointed ears still seems to be probable. I think so from the frequency of their occurrence and from the general correspondence in position with that of the tip of a pointed ear.

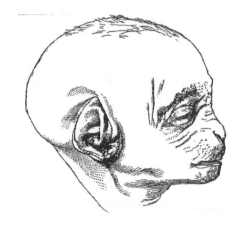

Fig. 3 Fetus of an orang. Exact copy of a photograph, showing the form of the ear at this early age.

The sense of smell is of the highest importance to the greater number of mammals –to some, as the ruminants, in warning them of danger; to others, as the Carnivora, in finding their prey; to others, as the wild boar, for both purposes. But the sense of smell is of extremely slight service, if any, even to the dark-coloured races of humans, in whom it is much more highly developed than in the white and civilised races.[5]

---

5   The account given by Humboldt of the power of smell possessed by the natives of South America is well known and has been confirmed by others. M??? Houzeau (*Etudes sur les Facultés Mentales, &c.* ??? i., 1872, p. 91) asserts that he repeatedly experiments and proved that Negroes could recognise persons in the dark. Dr. W. Ogle has made some ??? the connection between the colouring matter of the olfactory region as???have, therefore???coloured ra???white ra??? *Trans-???*

JACOB'S LAST STAND

IN COMPLIANCE WITH THE JUDGE's orders, the parties reconvened on April 13 for an extraordinary session. Judge Kuziora intended to see more than a typical day in which the accuser and the accused bring their finest tools for closing arguments. Since she was to decide the outcome of the trial and give the reasons for her ruling, Judge Kuziora wanted to get the most out of this litigation. She knew that to some degree, the case required reasoning in lieu of tangible evidence, as the origin of life at any level of complexity is something that cannot be imitated or reconstructed. Judge Kuziora had already noticed some serious flaws in the handling of the complaint by the prosecution. Now she needed to examine carefully the other party, so if any cracks were to be found, the judge would have the simple task of releasing Jacob with the warning not to lecture people with his personal views. So far, though, Jacob and his team presented so many elements of the case, and in a way that could not be mocked or rebuked, making the judge consider seriously the future of evolution by purpose.

After being sworn in, Jacob spoke. "The power of imagination is important to us, the human race. In children, it can make learning and recreation fun. In adults, it can help one lead a better life by focusing on things we may improve on. And inventions are the result of our imagination. Now when it comes to science – and what is taught as such – we ought to be careful not to get carried away and drift into the realm of imagination. Let me be specific about this. 'Universe' is a word—"

Razputin objected. "Your Honour, the universe is not at issue here. Can we—"

Judge Kuziora overruled the objection. "Science is in my background, and I want to get to the bottom of the conflict. Therefore, I will allow the witness to go on."

Jacob continued.

Thank you. My point is quite simple; "universe" is the word the English dictionary defines as, "all that exists, including the heavens, the galaxies and everything therein." Its original meaning, "the whole", by definition comprises everything big and small, whether we see it or not. It is, however, increasingly common – even by scientists – to replace the meaning of it so as to reduce it to merely a large place or to make it interchangeable with the word "world." The trend is so appallingly frequent that in science books, we can read fantasy-inspired stories describing multiple universes beyond our own. Such stories are impossible to even begin to demonstrate. But besides that lies the fact they are based on gross errors, as you all will see next.

Jacob unfolded a poster of a large photograph taken with the Hubble space telescope. It depicted many galaxies known to be millions of light-years away from one another. Jacob explained,

Because of the vast distance from one galaxy to another, it should be recognised that we do not know what the galaxies look like now. The closest one to our own, named Andromeda M31, is about two million light-years away, so we are viewing with our telescopes the image of M31 as it was two million years ago. There are other galaxies far more distant yet, five hundred million light-years away. And there are those thousands of millions of light-years away from us. We read in science reports fantastic ideas written by individuals who possess credentials, and they write things such as, "Because of the present position of the galaxies." In reality, this information is completely unknown to us due to the distance.

Before this point is dismissed, I just want to say that the star Alpha Centaurus is just four light-years from the sun. Using our fastest rockets, it would take astronauts fifty thousand years to get there. Let us all put the distance in the proper perspective, the real one. We know from physics, astronomy, and biology that things are always changing; nothing stays exactly the same forever. To try to deceive people using science fiction concepts is just as wrong as to show pictures of Hollywood stars taken fifty or sixty years ago. Undoubtedly, we would have to agree they have changed a great deal. As far as the universe is concerned, there is no way of knowing how those clusters look at present. But one thing we do know is that space seems infinite. However far we scan and aim, using the most sophisticated methods, no one has ever found an indication that space ends somewhere. This only confirms the dictionary's definition of "universe" instead of a nonsensical idea of large number of universes. The big bang theory is based on such faulty grounds, contrary to all principles and laws of nature, yet it is taught as real science.

Razputin called for permission to ask Jacob a question. The judge granted the request, and he asked, "So if the big bang never happened, how do you explain the existence of time, space, and matter?"

Space is room for matter to exist. The big bang claims space is expanding like a cake being baked. The error there is that cakes are matter not space. It is the same with the balloon analogy; a balloon can only expand if there is room for it. Time is not some tangible thing to grasp. It is a concept through which we organise our schedules, but it is based on the earth's movement, that, in turn, measures days and years. Time can be confusing, depending on where you are. If you fly from west to east, you can easily lose track of it. And leaving the planet, it would get worse. On Mercury or Venus, a day is almost as long as a year; because of their proximity to the sun, the force of rotation is slow. This is the other element to consider, and it is known to be abundant all over the universe. Gravity and electromagnetic force are invisible and never known to cease. That force is essential for life and for things to be, from the huge and awesome display of stars in a galaxy down to atomic configurations responsible for organic structures to develop.

Concerning the presence of matter mentioned by Mr. Razputin, no evidence has been found to make us think it somehow appeared however number of years ago. Antoine Lavoisier, founder of modern chemistry, declared that "Nothing is gained or lost; everything is transformed." Let us consider light – the visible form of energy – being likewise mysterious. Yet its existence is not conditioned by any time frame. Like gravity and electromagnetism, these elements, so vital to sustain life, are not subject to age-determination methods useful in our terrestrial affairs. Let us consider also the comets, huge chunks of matter orbiting in the dark for long periods … until they come close to the earth, igniting and becoming fireballs … and the leftovers from dead stars, mixing with gas and energised by gravity, eventually generating new stars. It is a process that could go on forever.

Curious, Razputin asked Jacob, "Sir, you are a believer, and I know that Genesis describes the beginning in a way that seems to fit the big bang. What do you say?"

"Genesis explains the beginning not of the universe but of the solar system. God is quoted there as saying, 'Let there be light,' meaning he spoke the sun into combustion. What the book teaches is that the Creator never had a day one. Many try to picture God as one of us, giving him the looks of an old man. But that is an absurdity, because infinity is his domain, hence the need for a mediator between us and him, namely Jesus Christ. Jesus came here on a mission for our sake, teaching us the way. His enemies demanded his sacrifice for our release. This is plain to see in view of the prophecies, which are nothing other than stipulations between God and the enemy who challenged him."

"So that was because of Adam and Eve. But they were in a perfect world until they rebelled against God. That's odd, wouldn't you agree, Mr. Kodnia?"

"There is a misinterpretation. The Bible neither calls Eden perfect nor suggests it was. How could it be so with the enemy lurking to set up a trap for the first humans who were just like kids, because they became victims of a lie. They did not know what a lie was until after. Our Creator cares so deeply that he accepted the challenge, leaving the rescue in the hands of the one he sent."

Scratching his head in bewilderment, Razputin asked "Mr. Kodnia, what tells you that God is without any doubt connected to science?"

There are a number of things, which were written thousands of years ago, and in those days must have made little or no sense. One of the main passages for me is found in Isaiah some 2,800 years ago, in which God says, "To whom can you liken me that I should be made his equal? raise your eyes high up and see … who has created these things? It is the One who brings forth the army of them, even by number, due to the abundance of dynamic energy, he also being vigorous in power, not one is missing." Another passage makes it clear that they knew the earth was round, not flat, as it was written, "There is One who is dwelling above the circle of the earth." That's something gentiles some two thousand years later did not realise – until Columbus. I just wish to stress that everyone is free to believe or not; it is a personal choice not to be forced. I am convinced beyond doubt that, just as no messenger is greater than his or her master, no part of anything created is greater than the one who made it. And by this principle, I find it completely logical for an agent of life – called God, Holy Spirit, or even natural selection – to be real, rather than suppose life is the result of an accident without intervention from any life-giving agent. This is why Darwin's works should be explained in classrooms and compared with other theories, such as creation, intelligent design, and genetic mutations. We can't afford to be insensitive or narrow-minded. Many people define success in a shallow way: being the top student, dating a lot of people, making ridiculous amounts of money, or scoring the highest IQ. I think of so many who have been blessed by a certain genetic mutation that produced an extra chromosome – or a fraction of it – resulting in a child with Down's syndrome. For those who have no insight, that could be seen as a calamity. We should ask ourselves, much like Darwin did in his reflections about repulsive acts committed by men and women, how each can achieve their full potential with dignity and with the honour that comes from the right mindset.

Judge Kuziora called her secretary, who handed over the original police report. Anya Kuziora examined it briefly before asking the prosecution and defence teams to approach the bench. Boris Razputin, Valentina Krashmanova, and Vladimir Tserkov stood in front of the judge as she addressed them. "From the looks of it, the prosecution doesn't stand the chance. There are no clear signs of inciting an audience to disorderly conduct … no riot … not even use of foul language. In fact, Jacob did not resist his arrest. What I'm looking at right now is a calm, elderly man about to be set free. The only issue for me to decide is whether I should sign a plain-chocolate release order or add a recommendation based on the merits of the case, submitting a copy to the EU Parliament in Brussels. This is why I have not dismissed Mr. Kodnia as witness. I will ask him to explain something to us concerning life and evolution. If I find his response convincing, I might become a supporter myself. That's all."

Turning to Jacob, Judge Kuziora said, "Mr. Kodnia, there is a gap that I would like to bridge regarding the origin of life; I'm quite aware of the problem this has been for scientists, including the ones who reject the possibility of design in view of the implications. And because I perceive that you must have studied all this quite tirelessly, I am interested in your opinion as to how life may have originated."

"I trust you all know there are no recipes by which the process of life from square one can be revealed. But I am persuaded to picture the beginning, based on solid clues, as a reaction to something." Jacob Kodnia stood and took a few steps toward the exhibit board.

With your permission, Your Honour, I will sidetrack briefly in order to answer your query with more clarity. Life is not an ordinary event. For ages, humankind tried to discover signs of extraterrestrial life, so far without results. This fact made scientists more curious about our world and the seemingly privileged status the earth was endowed with. Following intense studies in the fields of physics, astronomy, geology, mathematics, and biology, a list of the main conditions a planet must satisfy for life was created. Such basic conditions are

1. A system of planets orbiting a star within the galactic habitable zone.
2. The planet should orbit a G2 type star – average size – at a proper distance from the star.
3. The planet must be protected by some giant planets; in our system, those are Jupiter, Saturn, Uranus, and Neptune.
4. The planet's orbit must be nearly circular.
5. The planet must have an oxygen-rich atmosphere.
6. The planet must have adequate mass; in comparison with all the other planets, the earth's mass = 1.
7. The planet must be orbited by a large moon.
8. The planet must have a magnetic field.
9. The planet must have tectonic activity.
10. The planet must have water in liquid form to absorb the star's energy as well as to carry nutrients for its soil to be fertile; consequently, adequate temperature is also required.
11. Proper ratio of water and dry land is essential for life.
12. The planet must have a moderate rate of rotation.

Now, let us consider this stunning reality; if earth were orbiting closer to the sun, even just 5 percent closer, the temperature would reach deadly levels, about 800° F. This is similar to Venus. And only 5 percent farther away would cause a formation of clouds of carbon dioxide, rendering our planet sterile, much like Mars. It is quite evident that the list of basic conditions makes all other planets extremely inhospitable, and because of the fact that all attempts to locate a planet comparable to ours outside the solar system have failed, there is by now no question about the exceptional qualities of planet earth. This point would inevitably lead to wonder and to reason. Should we call life "some accident," being more aware of the long list of requisites, so many things, tangible and intangible, visible and invisible, and from microcosmos to stars. Speaking of stars, let's take for example what happens every second inside our star, the sun.

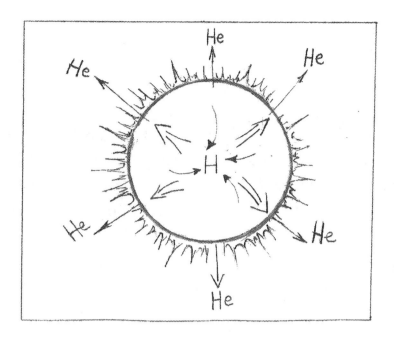

Over 500 million tons of hydrogen are transformed into more than 500 million tons of helium every second. This process is made by nuclear fusion inside the sun, releasing energy at proper levels for life here on earth.

Jacob paused for a moment so the data may sink in. Then he continued.

This process of massive transformation of energy has taken place innumerable times. This photograph, produced by the Hubble space telescope, is only a glimpse of what has been created. No one can actually count how many stars there are, not even the number of stars in the galaxies depicted by Hubble. Therefore, the amount of mass the universe holds, undergoing transformation or not, is simply impossible for us to calculate. This forces some proud and stubborn scientists to speculate, and that's how the big bang theory was conceived, reasoning it is impossible that amounts of mass and energy beyond what humankind can count or measure, along with space without boundaries, and time itself could have come from an explosion, which we know would require space. In addition, supporters of the theory have no clue as to what could cause a bang that supposedly made everything. Nor is anyone able to answer how far from the solar system such an explosion took place. We hear so often pretty much what students are taught just about everywhere, and all we see about creating life is some kind of accident or fluke. No design, no Creator, nothing directly responsible for all that exists. However, it is quite obvious that this "nothing" has a whole lot of something behind it.

The Milky Way

Our location in the galaxy
Distance: 100,000 light-years (diameter)

The solar system
Distance: 4 light-hours (from the sun to Neptune)

Assembly of Parts for a Purpose ⇨ Design

Irreducible Complexity
Bacteria Flagellum
A marvelous microscopic assembly of components, these
cellular structures are self-propelled thanks to their fantastic
design which comprises a rotor and a stator.

Jacob thanked the court for allowing his extracurricular testimony and continued.

Back to Darwin's evolution and his notion of all living things being evolved from a common ancestor through slight gradual modifications. Let us take one of nature's best friends, the honeybees. While Darwin offered a solid, rich analysis of the bees' construction methods, he never provided certain interesting facts about them. For example, bees store pollen by its colour so as to quickly identify any source later found not safe as food. By means of a circular dance, returning explorers are able to disclose the location of ingredients needed which more bees will help transport. The interior of the hive must be kept ventilated and clean. Some bees remain at the entrance, watching for invaders, such as moths, and blowing continuously. This evaporates excessive water that would otherwise mix with the food collected and stored. Bees keep blowing air over the nectar placed into cells. For about a century, it has been known that ten types of microorganisms responsible for illnesses like dysentery were destroyed within forty-eight hours when in contact with honey. This amazing quality was not understood until the 1960s, when it was demonstrated that in the making of honey, bees add a certain enzyme which reacts with the glucose in the honey to form hydrogen peroxide, a powerful germicide.

So how come they know all that? Random mutations causing them to fool around with chemical substances? Accident? I don't think so. These hard-working insects are quite connected – therefore vital – to a host of other species in the vegetable and animal kingdoms, including us. This truth can only lead me to believe in the reality of the life chain. That is, each species relies and depends on other species. Consequently, it is erroneous to think the variety of life forms – from plankton to trees, from gnats to human beings – is due to a process represented by an evolutionary tree never verified by fossil record, which allowed each species to develop up to a certain level before branching out to become a different species. Why not contemplate the possibility that evolution did take place within beings of the same species, but viewing life as a whole, they all had a purpose on this earth as one helps sustain another. By now, there is plenty of evidence that indicates quite clearly different life forms could not be the result of not evolving any further. Whoever buys into such an idea can only be considered narrow-minded. Different colours for our eyes to enjoy, different music notes for us to appreciate the arrangement of sounds. It is recreational, inspiring, and links us with the Maker.

Finally, to address the much-debated issue of origin of life, I would have to refer to a new branch of science, microbiology. I admit with complete honesty it is not my department. I rely on breakthroughs and what has been achieved so far. We all are more or less familiar with the tiny parts of the body that we call cells. They contain proteins that control genes, which in turn regulate the development of individuals according to what is available in terms of traits and overall characteristics. By lab testing and observation, it has been discovered that a certain type of bacteria has a hidden protein called repressor which, by binding to DNA sequence near the genes, causes the switching from one source of energy – glucose – to another – lactose. Thus genes are turned on and off by the flipping of genetic switches. Despite the progress made, it is yet to be understood how cell-to-cell communication is achieved. How signals are generated, transmitted, received, and interpreted remain, likewise, a mystery. But we know that time after time all genetic alterations attempted in labs resulted in gross distortions in development. For example, parts of a fly appear in unnatural areas of its body. But never ever once have changes been made that allow the branching into a different species, for instance, turning a fruit fly into a common fly. Darwin attributed variety of life forms to natural selection, but it doesn't get that far. A fly cannot become a different kind of fly, much less a honeybee; a moth cannot become a butterfly, just as an ape cannot become human. Bear in mind the fact that sea creatures share the environment but not their makeup. Dolphins are warm-blooded animals, and so are the whales as mammals. However, fish are not; they are cold-blooded and lay eggs.

Though similar DNA structures respond to proteins to activate genes for determined functions, there is no link found to this day, verifying the notion that genetic mutations –accidental or induced – would render a change from one species to another.

Judge Kuziora asked Jacob, "Then do you have an opinion regarding the first living structures?"

Again, I have to say this really isn't my cup of tea. But I dare to say that, in view of how the solar system was created and our planet so fine-tuned for life, living structures may have come in plurality, not as a single cell that oddly multiplied itself. Single cells stay as such. But if we consider that the world was shaped from a formless waste floating in the darkness into a dwelling place energised by the sun, once the conditions were in place, life flourished in many forms. More than that I cannot say. But I recognise Darwin, with his spot-on observations as well as his errors – such as the reversion idea which is the belief that, as Darwin put it, "The principle by which a long-lost structure is called back into existence – if man is descended from an apelike creature no valid reason can be assigned why certain muscles should not reappear suddenly after an interval of many thousand generations."

Darwin contradicts his own natural selection/sexual selection principle, because the NS/SS modifies structures for the good of the species. Reversion would imply that the selection process wasn't good after all. We know today that arrested development results more likely from occasional random genetic mutations. We know through DNA that genetic information would not disappear and reappear all of a sudden a thousand generations later. Genetics has determined that dominant and recessive traits exist, but recessive alleles tend to skip a generation or two. There's never a gap of the magnitude stated by Darwin, who never explained other issues without admitting first that he spoke in a speculative manner because of lack of solid proof, as is the case with the whole apelike progenitors of man choosing to walk on twos and becoming divested of body hair.

With that, I rest my case, Your Honour.

THE RULING

J UDGE KUZIORA CONTEMPLATED THE MATTER very carefully. For her, this was a journey that did not actually start with Jacob Kodnia's case. It had been revolving throughout her life, particularly in her growing up. She had felt torn by her vocational calling – science – and switching later to law school based on recommendations by people she loved and trusted the most. So there it was. Over twenty years after her difficult career decision, Anya Kuziora sat inside the judge's chambers, holding in her hands a heavy folder containing what would pave the road for new and better teaching methods in schools. Inside was evidence showing many souls that inspired expressions –including theories – should be tested, especially when a theory is somehow upgraded to the level that it is taught as fact. Taking a two-hour break, Judge Kuziora wrote her ruling, assisted by her secretary and both court reporters so that the document would emerge in English and Russian simultaneously. When the break was over, they returned to the courtroom to meet the parties. The media and general public filled hallways and staircases.

Addressing the prosecution team and the defence counsel, Judge Kuziora delivered her ruling.

> This has been a process that we are likely to remember. The case has been around for a century and a half, really. Jacob Kodnia may be seen as a clear example of the passions the controversy engenders. Are we to acknowledge a superior being for all that is created and exists or we refuse to imagine something – someone – greater than us, the human race, by saying there is no one, and this came about by mere chance, without any order or design? This is the heart of the matter, the core. In comparison to past litigations in the West, including the so-called Monkey Trial in the United States, this has been the boldest and most conclusive one. There have

been multiple instances of strong ties between what is observable through scientific methods and what is recorded in the Bible, noting the book is not to be considered a science text but a collection of testimonies offered to humankind for its benefit and surpassing in accuracy Darwin's teachings. Such is the case concerning human females and their development from young girl into adult woman. Three separate aspects were shown during the trial which Darwin proved inaccurate or missed completely.

1. Physical. Unwanted body hair grows, and it grows back after removal, regardless of the females' desire to be rid of it. This is known in all cultures and races. Female body hair is invariably perceived as a strong turn-off. Based on the NS/SS principles proposed by Darwin, this structurally unwanted feature that affects women negatively should have been resolved to improve on the physical attraction principle that gives way to progeny.

2. Emotional. The footage watched during the trial about the impressive magnetism of a popular singer among his female crowds points to a true quality known to civilisation since ancient times. That is, the females' emotional developmental capacity and natural inclination to belong to a male, to be craved by him. Also verified is the natural disposition of the female to compete for the male of her fancy.

3. Intellectual development. According to Darwin, man is intellectually superior by nature and so more able to achieve intellectually. Female detectives and female forensic technicians are living proof that Darwin's assumptions were wrong.

The law requires that a case be reviewed from the parties' standpoint, examining any material evidence as well as the testimony of witnesses to establish the relevant facts about the case. Because of the complexity of this case, the court is compelled to rely on elements of significant value introduced during the course of the trial and admitted into the record either by the prosecution team or by the defence. With the authority that is vested upon me by law here in Russia, I will mention all of the elements of importance, along with the court's decision on each whether to validate or reject them.

Judge Kuziora looked to her right, where the defence counsel and the defendant sat, and called out, "Mr. Jacob Kodnia, please stand." At once, Jacob sprung up.

Regarding the criminal charges filed against you by Moscow police last January, you've been found not guilty. Case dismissed. You may sit down now while I go on with the ruling concerning evolution and creation. And here it is.

- Resolution approved by the European Union banning the teaching of creationism in schools ... denied. This court does not endorse the EU's initiative in view of the merits of this case.

- Charles Darwin's biographical record ... verified.

- Darwin's principles of natural selection and sexual selection as the agencies involved in the species' adaptation to the environment ... verified.

- Darwin's hypothesis of apelike creatures as progenitors of man ... denied. Having examined Darwin's writings as well as what science offers today in the process of determining truth, there is no scientific evidence to accept the notion of humankind having evolved from apes without stepping into an area that requires faith, thus making such idea an issue of a religious nature, that is, to believe it with or without proof. Further, evolution from apelike creatures is presented by Darwin as speculative. It cannot be corroborated by means of any scientific methods, making it clearly an issue of faith, no more likely to be accurate than the Genesis account of how life originated. Hence, both evolution and creationism remain theories, *both* deserving their place in schools.

- Darwin's reversion principle … denied. It contradicts the NS/SS principles by definition. Darwin's concept of reversion is based on faulty grounds, being to some degree excusable considering the level of ignorance back in the nineteenth century. It is known today that the polymeric chromosomal constituent – called DNA – is formed by two long chains of alternating phosphate and deoxyribose units that are twisted into a double helix and joined by hydrogen bonds between complementary bases, each of which projects toward the axis of the helix from one of the strands, where it is bonded in a sequence that determines individual hereditary characteristics. It is recognised today that the tiny components of DNA strands can, however occasionally, alter the development of a structure by random mutation. So arrested development should not be attributed to a reversion but to an instance of random genetic mutation. Moreover, those with Down's syndrome are not, contrary to Darwin's thoughts about individuals with some developmental alterations, cases of reversion to some early progenitor of man. They have a genetic mutation that occurs randomly. And the notion of long-lost structures being called back into existence after a period of many thousand generations is imaginary nonsense, much like the idea, accepted by many back then, of light travelling through ether.

  I met a young girl who has one foot completely ordinary but the other showing the two smallest toes in switched positions, so the smallest toe actually precedes the one that normally comes before it. By Darwin's standards, it could be said this is arrested development by reversion. In truth, it is an alteration caused by random mutation.

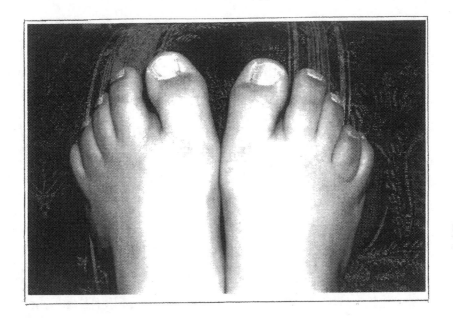

- Darwin's embryo models – drawings found in early editions of *The Descent of Man,* depicting a human embryo and that of a dog with the intention of making them equal … denied. Such aberration might have had some acceptance among Darwin's audience then, but it would never succeed in our world, certainly not here. It's no wonder that portion of *The Descent of Man* has been edited out.

- Developmental differences between humankind and apes … verified. The testimony during the trial afforded complete clarity on the huge chasm between the two at all levels of development. Just to add one more point here, I bear in mind a particular sensitivity – self-consciousness – humankind exhibits in reaction to nudity, by means of private parts exposed to shame. No other creature is made subject to such perception, not even the monkey.

- Darwin's hypothesis that humankind descends from apelike creatures who possessed large canine teeth, had hair covering the whole body, walked on all fours, and – both male and female – produced milk to nurse their offspring … denied. By lack of evidence, it is inadmissible in court and should not be taught in schools as science until it is proven through any scientific method. Having already established the huge differences between the two species, the burden of proof rests on those in support of the hypothesis. As it is presently, such an idea belongs in the realm of mythology, and it has its place there, similar to how we view and study constellations in the sky using ancient Greek mythology.

- Finally, the court finds sufficient and convincing cause after hearing both sides, evaluating their arguments in order to establish the facts, or at the very least, the likelihood of them. This court, accordingly, rejects the belief that nothing has played a role in the origin of life, calling it simply a natural accident. This court finds there is enough evidence to accept the notion of an agent of life as a source of life and its sustainer throughout the ages, observing the fact our world is indeed quite in tune for life to develop, and recognising that the cycle of life as we know it obeys certain rules, among which is that species depend on each other for their existence and livelihood. For this reason, scientists devoted to studying the environment feel strongly alarmed whenever a species is threatened to become extinct. This fact tends to confirm evolution by purpose is accurate.

Judge Kuziora concluded the ruling by announcing she was sending a recommendation to the EU Parliament, providing them with a complete copy of the transcripts for their review in order for them to reconsider its resolution to ban creationism from schools. Kuziora felt compelled to urge the EU not to be so hasty in accepting ideas that have not been verified, while prohibiting others that did not receive proper analysis. She specifically cited Genesis 1, not quite the way it was traditionally explained but in a way that greatly approaches what science has already discovered.

Judge Kuziora emphasised the importance of microbiology in assessing Darwin's ideas, adding that by doubting, progress is made and recognising scientists have the right to be wrong, because everyone makes mistakes. On the issue of the big bang theory, Kuziora stressed on the need for revisions in textbooks, as they present students with plenty of science fiction material as truth, citing the points made during the trial as the basis for necessary revisions.

In reference to the breakup of Pangaea during the formation of continents, she wrote about errors in the way students are instructed, offering the studies on this subject conducted by Liz McGillan and Wanda Newtowne, which the girls so willingly shared.

Anya Kuziora ended her report with the following reflection. "If we are not meant to experience love, how is it that we crave and hold onto the flame burning within us? In the same way, if we are not meant to seek and connect with that which is far greater than us – that which extends beyond our lives here – how is it that we cannot permanently ignore the longing in our hearts for truth, harmony, and unity?"

The courtroom doors swung open, and at last there he was: Jacob Kodnia, a free man, vindicated by overwhelming evidence in his favour. Crowds gathered in hallways to catch a glimpse of the man and the coalition, representing many. They were the silent majority, who patiently wait for answers … real answers. As Jacob was led by his team towards the lift, he noticed the monitor showing the verdict: Not Guilty. Then he noticed both prosecutors next to him, congratulating him on the outcome. "Your case leaves us thinking about things we thought we knew and about others we did not pay mind to before. Thank you, Mr. Kodnia," both of them said.

"I wish the best to the pair of you," Jacob said to Razputin and Krashmanova with a smile.

As for the coalition, it was a victory that called for a celebration, which was joined by many from that moment on.

APPENDIX A

The US Constitution vs. Separation of Church and State

The US constitution does not include any statement indicating a separation of church and state. There is only a reference to it made in a letter written by Thomas Jefferson. The reason for his doing so can be understood by looking at a map showing political divisions. In those days, European countries picked a specific church to be the one endorsed by the government. Consequently, many of their citizens were at risk by not being in agreement with the official church. Thomas Jefferson travelled through European countries, and understanding why the pilgrims had left Britain and drafted the Mayflower Compact on arrival in North America, he was determined to keep the new nation from becoming another country ruled by self-righteous leaders who would dispossess, persecute, and even kill people of different denominations.

Faith and worship are deeply rooted expressions of love in one's life, and even persons within the same congregation may differ greatly on. Seeking freedom in the new, independent land, Thomas Jefferson wanted Americans to live without having to hide, without having to call secret worship meetings to avoid official actions taken against them in the name of religion. The world had already seen enough of that. Violence and aggression are non-biblical measures, really, for it is from the Bible that we are commanded to treat others as we wish to be treated. "Whoever has ears to listen" is just an invitation which so often results in the joining of helpful men and women in the service of others. And yes, they assist victims of tragic events, offering their time, talents, and money so people in crisis may be comforted.

APPENDIX B

Down to the Bone

Some present-day scientists report that, based on the short size of bones thought to belong to ancient apes, it is possible to link them to the lineage of primates that eventually turned into humans. One problem with this concept, however, is that it is not consistent with the human race. Dwarfism is a well-known hereditary condition observed among people of various ethnic groups, including Caucasians, Africans, Asians, and Pacific Islanders. Moreover, in Africa alone we find the Watusi (giants) and the Pygmy (dwarfs), both groups being quite natural generation after generation. Therefore, "island dwarfing" as the cause of short stature due to lack of resources to sustain population seems rather inaccurate. With much speculation, it is reported that ' hobbits' shrank in response to lack of food. History shows that when a confined area such as an island no longer provides food for its inhabitants, they perish, as it happened at Easter island, Chile.

Reflections from the Author on the Human Genome

I have enjoyed the blessing of a large family, as well as having pets in my childhood; my black poodle was a real friend. I also had parrots. Those birds were quite alert and so clever that before long, they learned to talk. Some parrots are known for this skill, virtually unique in the animal kingdom. They can be very jealous creatures, something I found out the hard way. Growing up, I travelled by sea and visited many countries with amazingly exotic places where nature is seen first-hand.

Around 2007, members of the Human Genome Project ran some experiments to learn about our DNA in comparison with the genetic building blocks of other animals. Certain areas were located where rapid changes make a significant difference in an organism's functioning. The experiment led to gene sequencing being expressed in letters – T, G, C, and A. A snippet of 118 letters was obtained and named the Human Accelerated Region 1 (HAR1). In comparison, they said chimps differ from humans in eighteen of those sequencing letters, and hens differ from chimps by another two. HAR1 is thought to be important regarding changes from one species to another.

FOXP2 is another important gene, containing fast-changing sequences involved in human speech. Scientists in Europe reported recently that Neanderthals had a modern version of FOXP2, adding that this speech-enabling gene would have allowed Neanderthals to talk like we do. They went on to report that what makes human speech so distinguished from vocal communication in other animals does not come from physical means but from cognitive ability, correlated to brain size that in humans tripled the size of chimp-human ancestors some six million years ago. The article, which appeared in Scientific American, indicates a common ancestor of human and hen existed three hundred million years ago.

After reading this, I thought about my parrots, so smart by nature. Using the rationale employed by Darwinian evolution, it becomes apparent some things do not make sense here. The fact that in a short period of time parrots can learn human speech implies that natural selection somehow decided to deprive all animals except parrots from the ability to talk. Incidentally, the DNA sequencing cites several kinds of animals, but no parrots. I can't help but wonder why parrots and not dogs, horses, or apes as our direct ancestors? Something to ponder.

Claiming my right to invoke reasonable doubt, I question the issue of a so-called common ancestor of human and hen dating back three hundred million years. I examined the geological periods which indicate what changes took place on earth and how long ago. It can be noticed that Trilobites populated the planet for about 270 million years, undergoing minor changes during such a mind-boggling lengthy time from the early Cambrian to the mid-Permian, that is, within the period in which there was supposedly a common ancestor of human and chicken. It can also be observed this is shortly before the dinosaur domination that lasted some 180 million years, from the Triassic through the beginning of the Paleozoic period. It does not seem likely such a creature existed three hundred million years ago, minding the fact that many radical genetic changes would have been required. Without solid hard evidence, there is really no reason to accept this type of idea any more than anything else offered as an explanation for the richness in life forms that our planet brings.

In memory of Jacob Kodnia, my grandfather